Wilton House and
English Palladianism

Ea: of Pembrock: Wilton   Great Roome.

1649.

211:

1: foote.

ROYAL
COMMISSION
ON THE HISTORICAL
MONUMENTS
OF ENGLAND

Wilton House and English Palladianism

Some Wiltshire Houses

JOHN BOLD
with John Reeves

LONDON: HER MAJESTY'S STATIONERY OFFICE

ISBN 0 11 300022 7
1005445353

Printed in the United Kingdom
for Her Majesty's Stationery Office
Dd. 240056 8/88 C20

HMSO publications are available from:

HMSO Publications Centre
(Mail and telephone orders only)
PO Box 276, London, SW8 5DT
Telephone orders 01-622 3316
General enquiries 01-211 5656
(queuing system in operation for both numbers)

HMSO Bookshops
49 High Holborn, London, WC1V 6HB   01-211 5656 (Counter service only)
258 Broad Street, Birmingham, B1 2HE   021-643 3740
Southey House, 33 Wine Street, Bristol, BS1 2BQ   (0272) 264306
9-21 Princess Street, Manchester, M60 8AS   061-834 7201
80 Chichester Street, Belfast, BT1 4JY   (0232) 238451
71 Lothian Road, Edinburgh, EH3 9AZ   031-228 4181

HMSO's Accredited Agents
(see Yellow Pages)

and through good booksellers

Frontispiece
John Webb. Design for composite capital for
the overmantel of the Great Dining Room
(the Double Cube Room), 1649, depicting the
Herbert wyvern flanked by cornucopias.
(*Book of Capitols*, Devonshire Collection,
Chatsworth)

Contents

Illustrations

Introduction

Wilton House

Amesbury Abbey

Wilbury House

Stourhead

Tottenham Park

Lydiard Park

Commissioners

The Right Honourable the Earl Ferrers
Maurice Warwick Beresford, Esq
Martin Biddle, Esq
Richard Bradley, Esq
Robert Angus Buchanan, Esq
Bridget Katherine Cherry
John Kerry Downes, Esq
John Davies Evans, Esq
Richard David Harvey Gem, Esq
Sir Harry Thurston Hookway, Kt
Derek John Keene, Esq
Peter Erik Lasko, Esq , CBE
Geoffrey Haward Martin, Esq , CBE
Gwyn Idris Meirion-Jones, Esq
Antony Charles Thomas, Esq
Malcolm Todd, Esq

Secretary
Tom Grafton Hassall, Esq

Chairman's Preface

The preparatory work for this study was carried out by the investigative staff of the Royal Commission's Salisbury office. During the course of work on a wide range of domestic buildings, it became apparent that the material existed for a volume on Palladian houses, which could show how local examples of such houses fitted into the national picture.

The publication of a book, which takes architectural style and patronage as its theme, but which is based on an examination of buildings and documents, is a new departure for the Royal Commission. It is a reflection of the Royal Commission's intention to produce publications, the form and approach of which can be varied according both to the subject and to the type of evidence.

The Commissioners would like to thank all those who have worked on the project, particularly John Reeves and his colleagues in the Salisbury office, who were responsible for the initial investigation of the houses. Their thanks also go to Dr John Bold, who added much material of his own, which has served to broaden the scope of the volume. It indicates the extent to which these buildings reflect a national pattern.

Whilst the Commissioners have given help and advice on the writing of the manuscript, the views which are expressed are those of the author. The Commissioners are particularly grateful for the generous co-operation which has been provided by the owners of the houses which have been recorded.

Fuller details and supplementary material on the buildings which have been recorded are available to the public in the National Monuments Record, Royal Commission on the Historical Monuments of England, 23 Savile Row, London W1X 2JQ.

FERRERS

Notes and Acknowledgements

The plans and elevations of the three houses studied here in detail are taken from RCHME surveys made between 1978 and 1980. Unless otherwise indicated, the drawings have been produced to a scale of eight feet to the inch.

Within the text, linear dimensions are expressed in imperial units: a guide to metric equivalents is given below:

1 inch = 25.4 mm

1 foot (12 inches) = 304.8 mm

1 yard (3 feet) = 914.4 mm

1 mile (1760 yards) = 1.6 km

Bold numbers contained within square brackets refer to illustrations. A complete list of illustrations can be found on pages vi–viii.

A number of abbreviations have been used within the text:

BL   British Library
HBMC   Historic Buildings and Monuments Commission
HMSO   Her Majesty's Stationery Office
RCHME   Royal Commission on the Historical Monuments of England
RIBA   Royal Institute of British Architects
VCH   Victoria History of the Counties of England
WAS   Wiltshire Archaeological Society
WAM   Wiltshire Archaeological and Natural History Society Magazine
WHA   Wilton House Archives
WRO   Wiltshire Record Office

All photographs are copyright of RCHME, with the exception of the following, which are reproduced by permission:

Bodleian Library: 43, 84, 126, 149

Dr J Bold: 175

British Library: 42

Chatsworth Settlement Trustees: frontispiece, 56, 137, 207, 208, 209

Country Life: 81, 216

Courtauld Institute of Art: frontispiece, 4, 30, 31, 33, 34, 35, 36, 48, 49, 50, 51, 57, 59, 111, 137, 150, 207, 208, 209

Freeman and Co, London: 106

A F Kersting: 17

Metropolitan Museum of Art, New York: 142, 145

Foreword

The compilation of this book has been, in large measure, collaborative, and I wish to thank all those who have contributed. The initial investigation of the three houses was carried out by John Reeves and Nicholas Moore of the Royal Commission's Salisbury office, and documentary research in the Wilton House archives was carried out by Dr Bridgett Jones. John Reeves also has been responsible for the elevation and comparative drawings, and Nigel Fradgley has produced the plans and the cut-away view of Amesbury. Photography has been carried out by Peter Williams and by Ron Braybrook, whilst the printing of older photographs from the RCHME archives has been the responsibility of Tony Rumsey and the staff in the photographic department. I also wish to thank other colleagues in the Commission, particularly John Smith and Stephen Croad, for their encouragement of the project and Rosalind Woodhouse for her sympathetic editing of the text.

Outside the Royal Commission, my debts are firstly to Lord Pembroke, Lady St Just and the late Lord St Just, and Mrs E M Cornelius Reid for allowing access to their houses, and secondly to those curators, archivists and librarians who have done much to enable the necessary documentary work to be undertaken: the staff of the Drawings Collection of the RIBA, the staff of the Wiltshire Record Office, the staff of the Bodleian and British Libraries, and Mrs Lesley Le Claire at Worcester College, Oxford.

Lastly, I wish to thank those constructive critics of the text in its various stages who have discussed the subject with me at length and have contributed significantly to the final product: Dr Robin Evans, John Harris, Richard Hewlings, Gordon Higgott, Professor George Knox, and particularly, Professor Kerry Downes, who has provided unfailing support throughout the period of the project.

John Bold

The Royal BANQUETING-HOUSE in Whitehal.

1 Banqueting House, Whitehall. A late seventeenth-century engraving of Inigo Jones's building of 1619–22. (*Wren Society* **VII**, 1930, pl **XII**)

Introduction

The present study is occasioned by the Royal Commission's recent investigation of three important Palladian houses in Wiltshire: Wilton, Amesbury and Wilbury. The study seeks to place them in the broader context of the national style and to amplify some of the issues raised by reference to three further stylistically comparable Wiltshire houses: Stourhead, Tottenham Park and Lydiard Park. Lydiard was fully investigated by the Commission some years ago and the investigators' findings formed the basis of the published guidebook to the house. The accounts of Stourhead and Tottenham are based upon published sources rather than upon investigation of the present fabric of the houses.

Although the Palladian style continued in fashionable use in Wiltshire, as elsewhere in the country, after the mid eighteenth century, we are concerned here with its early development, so Alderman Beckford's vanished Fonthill Splendens of *c.* 1757 and the 8th Lord Arundell's Wardour Castle, designed by James Paine and begun in 1770, fall outside the scope of the present study.

Whilst we are laying particular stress upon the Palladian aspects of these houses, it clearly is desirable to review their architectural histories in full, not least because of the contributions made to those histories by nineteenth-century architects of national importance. The historical accounts therefore deal with the histories of the houses from their foundation up to the present century.

English Palladianism customarily is defined as the architectural style which is derived from the works of the sixteenth-century Italian architect, Andrea Palladio, introduced to English Court circles by Inigo Jones in the early seventeenth century, and continued by his pupil, John Webb. The style was not based purely upon Palladio's own works. It was enriched firstly by the example of classical antiquity, which both Palladio and Jones had studied in Italy, and secondly by the work of Palladio's follower, Vincenzo Scamozzi. This first Palladian phase, which came to an end with the death of John Webb in 1672, must be distinguished from the early eighteenth-century Palladian revival which was conceived as a reaction to much of the architecture of the later seventeenth century and was based not only on Palladio, Scamozzi and Roman antiquity, but also on the works of Jones and Webb themselves. This later style is designated neo-Palladianism.

2 A Palladio, *I Quattro Libri dell'Architettura*: title page of first edition, 1570 (*see* p 6)

The National Context

The rise of English neo-Palladianism was a triumph of propaganda and politics. From its uncertain beginnings in aristocratic Whig circles during the early years of the reign of George I, it had become by the 1730s the established style for both country houses and public buildings. Curiously, given its naming, its development owed as much to the example of Inigo Jones as it did to Palladio and it had as much to do with John Webb as it did with Jones. Although we can plot a line of historical development from Palladio's Venice in 1570 to London in *c.* 1720, the evidence for the early eighteenth-century genesis of neo-Palladianism in England is somewhat circumstantial. The prime movers were to be Colen Campbell, Giacomo Leoni and the 'Apollo of the Arts', Lord Burlington, but it was the 3rd Earl of Shaftesbury who had first expressed the sentiments which in the absence of any other theoretical justification must stand as the most significant plea for a new and appropriate national architectural style.

Shaftesbury, ailing in Naples, completed his *Letter concerning the Art or Science of Design* in March 1712. It was sent to London, to Lord Somers, and although it did not appear in print until the fifth edition of *Characteristicks* in 1732, having been suppressed by its author's executors, it seems likely that it was circulated in manuscript.[1] The *Letter* attacked 'one single Court-architect', the unnamed Sir Christopher Wren, throughout whose Surveyorship of the Works, 'through several reigns we have patiently seen the noblest public buildings perish'. However, he continued, 'It is the good fate of our nation in this particular, that there remain yet two of the noblest subjects for architecture; our Prince's Palace and our House of Parliament . . . Our State, in this respect, may prove perhaps more fortunate than our Church, in having waited till a national taste was formed before these edifices were undertaken.'[2]

Shaftesbury did not venture how a national taste might be made manifest in a national architectural style, but earlier in his *Letter* he offered a clue, when he suggested that 'our genius . . . will naturally carry us over the slighter amusements, and lead us to that higher, more serious, and noble part of imitation, which relates to history, human nature, and the chief degree or order of beauty; I mean that of the rational life, distinct from the merely vegetable and sensible, as in animals or plants'.

Thus the need was stated for an architectural style which could be perceived as being at once national and rational,

3 Queen's House, Greenwich: the south front. Designed by Inigo Jones; begun in 1616–19 for Queen Anne of Denmark and completed between 1630 and 1635 for Queen Henrietta Maria. (Colen Campbell, *Vitruvius Britannicus*, i, 1715)

and, incidentally, as unlike the baroque classicism of Wren and Hawksmoor as possible. Two years after Shaftesbury's death, Colen Campbell took up the point in the first volume of *Vitruvius Britannicus, or the British Architect*. Published in 1715, with further volumes appearing in 1717 and 1725, this lavish folio presented a sumptuous view of a century of British architectural achievement, which appeared to culminate in recent designs by Campbell himself. Buildings of the English baroque were among those illustrated, but in his short introduction Campbell stated his true position and made his purpose clear:

The general Esteem that Travellers have for things that are Foreign, is in nothing more conspicuous than with Regard to Building. We travel, for the most part, at an Age more apt to be imposed upon by the Ignorance or Partiality of others, than to judge truly of the Merit of Things by the Strength of Reason. It's owing to this Mistake in Education, that so many of the British Quality have so mean an Opinion of what is performed in our own Country; tho', perhaps, in most we equal, and in some Things we surpass, our Neighbours.[3]

Campbell acknowledged the 'very great Obligations' which we have to 'those Restorers of Architecture, which the Fifteenth and Sixteenth Centurys produced in Italy. . . . above all the great Palladio, who has exceeded all that were gone before him, and surpass'd his Contemporaries', seeming 'to have arrived to a Ne plus ultra of his Art'. But, echoing the sentiments expressed in 1646 by the weary Lord Arundel that 'Italy was no more Italy',[4] he found that seventeenth-century Italian architecture had lost its way and was devoid of proportion, grace and symmetry: 'How

Extends 115

a Scale of 60 Feet.

The Elevation of the QUEENS House to the Park at GREENWICH Invented by Inigo Iones 1639.
is most humbly Inscribed to the Hon.ble GEORGE CLARKE Esq.r One of the Lords of the Admiralty. &c.

Elevation D'une Maison appartenante a La REINE. Du Costé Du Parc a GREENWICH tres humblement Dedié a Monsieur M.r CLERC. &c.

affected and licentious are the works of Bernini and Fontana? How wildly Extravagant are the Designs of Boromini, who has endeavoured to debauch Mankind with his odd and chimerical Beauties'.

Campbell's was the language of polemic rather than of exposition, and in true campaigning style he went on to present his audience with an English champion to set in the 'lists' opposite Palladio, making the bold claim that 'an impartial Judge' would find in the work of Inigo Jones all the regularity of Palladio 'with an Addition of Beauty and Majesty, in which our Architect is esteemed to have out-done all that went before'.

For Campbell's generation, Inigo Jones represented an idea and a focus. Classicism, fostered by continental pattern books, had appeared in English architecture before Jones, but he was the first to apply the classical principles of architecture as a thoroughgoing system of design which permeated all aspects of a building, rather than treating classical details as a species of applied motifs. His Banqueting House in Whitehall [1] was a deeply considered Italianate masterpiece, the product of a Court-based architecture which demanded academic rigour and enlightened patronage, and found its principal outlet through the Royal Works [3, 4]. Charles I recognised the sophistication of the style and the singularity of his architect, and encouraged Jones to train a successor. John Webb was, by his own statement, 'brought up by his Unckle Mr. Inigo Jones upon his late Maiestyes command in the study of Architecture, as well that wch relates to building as for masques, Tryumphs and the like'.[5] But the continuity of the Royal Works was shattered by the Civil War and the Interregnum and, at the Restoration, Webb's expectations were unfulfilled as the Surveyorship eluded him.

Webb was England's first trained professional architect, with a far larger country house building practice than Jones. It was his failure to achieve high

4 Prince's Lodging, Newmarket. Alternative designs by Inigo Jones for the façade, *c*. 1619 to *c*. 1621; demolished *c*. 1650. (RIBA Drawings Collection)

office which in part explains why he seems never to have emerged from Jones's considerable shadow. Roger North, writing towards the end of the seventeenth century, was able to distinguish the individual contributions of the two men, but by the time of Campbell, Webb's role had been subsumed within that of Jones.[6] So it was that the two proto-Palladian villas *par excellence*, Gunnersbury House [5, 6] and Amesbury Abbey, designed and built by Webb, were both credited in *Vitruvius Britannicus* to the master rather than to the pupil.

Palladio himself had no need of Campbell's championship. Since its first publication in Venice in 1570, his *Quattro Libri dell' Architettura* [2] had been an enduring success, with four reprints being made from the original wood blocks in

1581, 1601, 1616 and 1642. Both Inigo Jones and John Webb owned and annotated copies of the 1601 edition. (Now in the library of Worcester College, Oxford.) Webb's had been rebound with an interleaved manuscript translation into English, but no published edition in English was available until a century later. An English version of *Book I*, on the Orders, appeared in 1663, translated by Godfrey Richards 'for an assistance to our Ingenious Workmen, and Improvement of English Architecture'. This it attempted to be through twelve editions until far into the eighteenth century.[7] The plates and additional text on doors and windows were taken by Richards from Le Muet's French edition of *Book I*, published in 1645. A complete French edition had been issued in a translation by Fréart de Chambray in 1650.

5   Gunnersbury House, Middlesex: the south front. Designed by John Webb and built *c.* 1658 to *c.* 1663 for Sir John Maynard; demolished 1801. (Colen Campbell, *Vitruvius Britannicus*, I, 1715)

The Elevation of GUNNERSBURY House near BRANTFORD in the County of MIDDLESEX by Inigo Iones.

The appeal of the *Quattro Libri* lay in its attractive layout, its numerous illustrations of actual buildings, including their plans, and its straightforward, practical text. It combined the virtues of the architectural pattern book with those of the learned treatise, omitting both the more fanciful elements of the former and the discursive elements of the latter to achieve an elegant, lucid synthesis.

The first complete English translation of the *Quattro Libri* to be published appeared in parts between 1715 and 1720. This edition was every bit as lavish as Campbell's book and its author, Giacomo Leoni, like Campbell, clearly hoped for architectural patronage as a result. Leoni was a Venetian who had come to England *c.* 1713 from the Court of the Elector Johann-Wilhelm of the Palatinate at Düsseldorf. He was perhaps following a suggestion of his fellow Venetian, the painter Giovanni Antonio Pellegrini, who arrived at the Court of the Elector in the summer of 1713, after having worked in England since 1708 at Kimbolton, Castle Howard and Burlington House.[8] It is possible that upon his arrival in London, Leoni solicited the assistance of the young Lord Burlington, who was shortly to employ another Venetian, Sebastiano Ricci, on the painting of the mythologies which decorated James Gibbs' new staircase at Burlington House.[9] Certainly, Ricci subsequently designed the allegorical frontispiece for Leoni's edition of Palladio, the translation being provided by Nicholas Dubois, whom Leoni had first met in Düsseldorf. Both Leoni and Dubois were subsequently involved in building projects on the Burlington

6 Gunnersbury House, Middlesex: plans of the ground and first floors. (Colen Campbell, *Vitruvius Britannicus*, I, 1715)

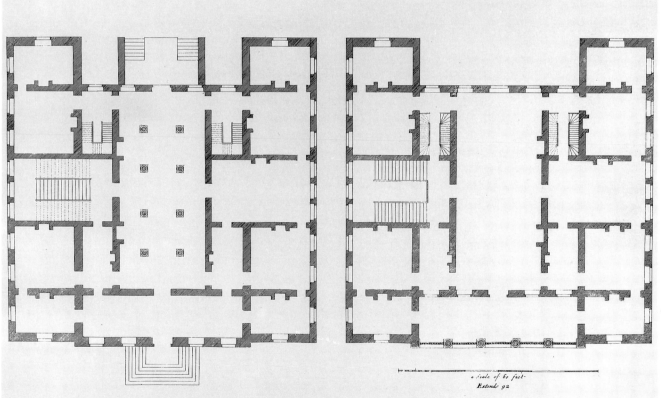

The plan of y first story of Gunnersbury house
Plan du premier Estage de la Maison De Gunnersbury

The plan of y principall floor of Gunnersbury
Plan du principal Estage de la maison de Gunnersbury

estate in London, with Leoni designing Queensberry House for Burlington's first cousin, the Duke of Queensberry, who was to become the owner of Amesbury Abbey.

Leoni was quick to catch the mood of the moment, not only in publishing Palladio, a project upon which probably he had been working for some time, but also in promoting the work of Inigo Jones. In 1715, he advertised his intention of publishing the 'notes and remarks' which Jones had made in his own copy of the *Quattro Libri*, but he was not able to fulfil this promise until the third edition of the book, which appeared in 1742. This move was not merely opportunist, for throughout his career, Leoni's designs displayed his considerable indebtedness to the work of Jones.[10]

Leoni's *Quattro Libri* was clearly a success, running, despite competition, to three editions in the space of a little over twenty years. This success inspired him in a further publishing venture, an edition of Alberti's theoretical text, *Ten Books on Architecture*, in 1726. His version of Palladio was, on his own admission, not a faithful copy of the original text, but 'made so many necessary corrections with respect to shading, dimensions, ornaments etc. that this work may in some sort be rather considered as an Original than an Improvement'. The significance of Leoni's alterations has been exaggerated. In fourteen of the fifty-eight plates of villas in *Book II* he added and amended in generally minor particulars; he also added to *Book II* a plate of a plan and elevation of a villa, and to *Book III* a plan and elevation of the Roman Temple of Piety, both taken from de Chambray's edition.

These alterations were to be cited by Isaac Ware in the 'Advertisement' to his edition of the *Quattro Libri* [12] which he brought out with the patronage of Lord Burlington in 1738, and it usually has been presumed that the Leoni embellishments so inflamed the archaeologically inclined Burlington that he was driven to

prompt this faithful edition twenty years later. However, Burlington's initial opinion of Leoni's efforts appears to have been one of approval. Indeed, it was probably the combination of the publicity programmes of Leoni and Colen Campbell which prompted Burlington's interest in Palladio's architecture in the first place. On his Grand Tour to Italy in 1714–15, he had favoured Rome and spent only a short time in the Veneto. It was not until he travelled again to Italy in 1719 that he went specifically to study Palladio's work.[11] As a subscriber to Leoni's edition and as a patron who recommended the Venetian as an architect to his kinsmen in the 1720s, any disapprobation which Burlington felt towards the edition of Palladio could not have been immediate.

Leoni's was a publication for patrons rather than a builder's handbook. Colen Campbell attempted to fill the gap in the artisan market by producing, in 1729, a faithful edition of Palladio's *Book I:* to replace the Richards edition, which he entitled *Andrea Palladio's Five Orders of Architecture*. This was 'Faithfully Translated, and all the Plates exactly copied from the First Italian Edition . . . To which are added, Five Curious Plates of Doors, Windows, and Chimney-Pieces, invented by Mr Campbell'. This book does not appear to have sold well, being advertised still ten years later, but the material achieved a wider circulation through being incorporated by Halfpenny into his *Modern Builder's Assistant* of 1742.

By the mid 1730s Leoni's copyright had expired, and a pirated version of his Palladio was issued by Edward Hoppus and Benjamin Cole, who also drew on Campbell's *Five Orders*, and included chimney-pieces by Inigo Jones. It was probably the presumptuous dedication to 'the most Noble Lord Richard Boyle Earl of Burlington and Cork etc' which spurred Burlington into sponsoring Ware's edition.[12] Ware did not name Hoppus and Cole in his 'Advertisement', but his meaning was clear when he referred to the work which had been 'done with so little understanding, and so much negligence, that it cannot but give great offence to the judicious, and be of very bad consequence in misleading the unskilful'.

Although Burlington's example and his patronage were crucial for the development of neo-Palladianism, he did not embark upon a coherent publishing programme. Following Campbell in his enthusiasm for both Palladio and Inigo Jones, he succeeded in acquiring important groups of drawings by both architects: the Palladio drawings which Inigo Jones had bought in Italy in 1614, and the drawings of Roman baths which he purchased himself in 1719, as well as the large collection of drawings by Inigo Jones and John Webb which he bought from John Talman in 1720–1.[13]

These drawings provided the material for a group of occasional publications, beginning with William Kent's *Designs of Inigo Jones* in 1727. This included a substantial number of drawings by John Webb as well as drawings by Jones, all redrawn for the engraver by Burlington's protégé, Henry Flitcroft. A large group of the drawings, first published here, for the projected Whitehall Palace, were from the collection of George Clarke in Oxford. Further volumes of Jones and Webb material, together with designs by Kent and Burlington himself, were published by Isaac Ware as *Designs of Inigo Jones and Others* in 1733, and by John Vardy as *Some Designs of Mr Inigo Jones and Mr William Kent* in 1744. A selection of Palladio's drawings of Roman baths was published in 1730 as *Fabbriche Antiche disegnate da Andrea Palladio*.

All of these books were published after the first wave of neo-Palladian building activity. They were designed to appeal to connoisseurs rather than to builders, being attractive picture books rather than theoretical or expository texts, but they did prove to be mines of information for more popular writers who combed them for Jonesian details. These were then re-presented to the building trades,

divorced from context in a way which was wholly antithetical to those principles of thoroughgoing classicism which Jones represented.

Theoretical writings on architecture in England in the seventeenth and eighteenth centuries were few compared with the large number of practical books on details and, pre-eminently, on the Orders. There was a spate of such publications in the 1650s and 1660s, in the early years of the eighteenth century and again between the mid 1720s and the mid 1760s. During this last period, there was a particular concentration on the production of popular books for builders by such authors as Batty Langley, William Halfpenny, William Salmon, Francis Price and Edward Hoppus, which borrowed and adapted details and instructions from the available French and Italian treatises and pattern books, as well as pirating from each other. These popularisers were instrumental in the dissemination of an impure, artisan Palladianism in the provinces, for which they relied as much on the example of Vincenzo Scamozzi as they did upon that of Palladio.

Scamozzi, a follower of Palladio, designed a handful of buildings which were to be of outstanding importance for the seventeenth and eighteenth-century Palladians. These were illustrated in his large theoretical textbook, *L'Idea dell'architettura universale*, the last of the great Italian Renaissance treatises. It was never fully published in English, although manuscript versions were produced, but it was cannibalised regularly for its codification of the Orders, a frequently reprinted catchpenny edition being William Fisher's translation from the Dutch: *The Mirror of Architecture: or the Ground Rules of the Art of Building, exactly laid down by Vincent Scamozzi Master Builder of Venice*. This comprised a wholly disparate collection of illustrations from Scamozzi, a condensed text taken from Henry Wotton's *Elements of Architecture* and, in later editions, a 'diagonal scale for dividing Parts into Minutes' and the description of the 'Joynt Rule for finding lengths and angles of rafters . . . and drawing the architrave, frieze and cornice in any order', all for the benefit of those with 'ordinary Capacities'. First published in 1669, the *Mirror of Architecture* ran to six further editions before 1708.[14]

Books on house planning were fewer. Outside the Palladian circle, James Gibbs published 150 plates of his own designs in 1728 in *A Book of Architecture*, which was designed to fulfil the requirements of both patrons and builders, but apart from this singular contribution, there were no readily accessible books of plans in English available to builders and craftsmen before the 1750s. The *Vitruvius Britannicus*, the editions of Palladio, and the designs of Jones and Webb, were intended for the patrons only, and those of 'meaner capacities' and purses had to wait until plans received overdue attention from William Halfpenny and, less cheaply, from such men as Abraham Swan, John Aheron and Isaac Ware. Ware is of particular interest in this context because we might expect from him, given the fidelity of his edition of the *Quattro Libri*, a canonical justification of Palladian practice, but by the time of the appearance of his *A Complete Body of Architecture* in 1756, the moment of neo-Palladianism was past and he was able to offer criticisms of the master in the light of national conditions and expectations. Indeed, his published plans are more indebted to the established English type, the double pile, than they are to the Palladian villa.

Given the eloquence and general utility of Palladio's own text, it is perhaps not surprising, especially in a country as determinedly empirical as England, that theoretical expositions of neo-Palladianism were not produced by the architects and patrons of its first phase. Theory followed practice, and it was not until 1728, in *An Essay in Defence of ancient Architecture*, that such an attempt at codification was made. In it, Robert Morris, the younger cousin of the architect Roger Morris, launched a vigorous attack on the baroque style for what he perceived as an absence of truth and reason, without which, he averred, there could be no beauty. In his subsequent *Lectures on Architecture*, published in 1734, he laid further stress on this point and expatiated on the subject of 'harmonic' proportions towards the conclusion summarised in a useful, recent account of his theory: 'There could be no beauty without the truthful obedience to natural laws; laws of proportion, harmony, regularity which had been formulated by the ancients from an observation of nature and passed onto the present age by the good offices of Palladio'.[15]

The diagrammatic quality of Palladio's illustrations in the *Quattro Libri* certainly renders them particularly open to geometrical analysis and exegesis, but an important inquiry into Palladio's use of harmonic proportions has demonstrated that, although his work displayed a clear preference for 'harmonic' numbers, that is, multiples of two, three and five, the pages of the *Quattro Libri* 'betray no coherent underlying system which could have governed Palladio's principles of design'. This inquiry also comes to the significant conclusion that 'in most cases there is little evidence of conscious idealisation of the proportions of the actual buildings for the purpose of publication'.[16]

But in the illustrations in the *Quattro Libri*, Palladio did provide models which were self-evidently divorced from their contexts. Their planar precision, accentuated in the English editions by their translation from woodcut to copperplate, appears to have conditioned the response of most of his imitators, especially those who did not have the privilege of visiting the buildings themselves and thus experiencing them in all their three-dimensional, volumetric splendour. Those like Vasari who did not see Palladio through the medium of the *Quattro Libri* did not view him as the chaste, classical purist which he became for later generations.[17]

This two-dimensional mode of looking was brought to bear also by the English neo-Palladians on buildings by Inigo Jones and John Webb. In *Vitruvius Britannicus*, Campbell flattened and refined those features which he found to be incompatible with his own taste; thus, the façade of Jones's Banqueting House appears far blander in his engraving [7] than it did in earlier representations; the proportions of the river front of Somerset House are adjusted; Gunnersbury and Amesbury lose their idiosyncratic composite capitals; Chevening loses its block cornice, and so on. This way of seeing lay behind the development by neo-Palladian architects of the anti-baroque compositional technique which has come to be known as 'concatenation', in which the façades of the building were composed of discrete yet related elements set in different planes. Thus we find in the most ambitious of English neo-Palladian buildings a staccato quality which is entirely new; absent from the work of Palladio and Jones alike, and absent also from the work of the large number of provincial imitators who used the received forms in a purely decorative manner, so that we may say, borrowing from Leoni, that the buildings 'may in some sort be rather considered as an Original than an Improvement'.

This approach to design can best be appreciated by comparing the supreme example of the neo-Palladian house, Holkham Hall [8], with the masterpiece of the English baroque, Blenheim Palace [9]. Vanbrugh's was an architecture of movement and rhetoric. At Blenheim, he

7 Banqueting House, Whitehall. Colen Campbell's illustration of the façade; (*Vitruvius Britannicus*, I, 1715) *see* **1**

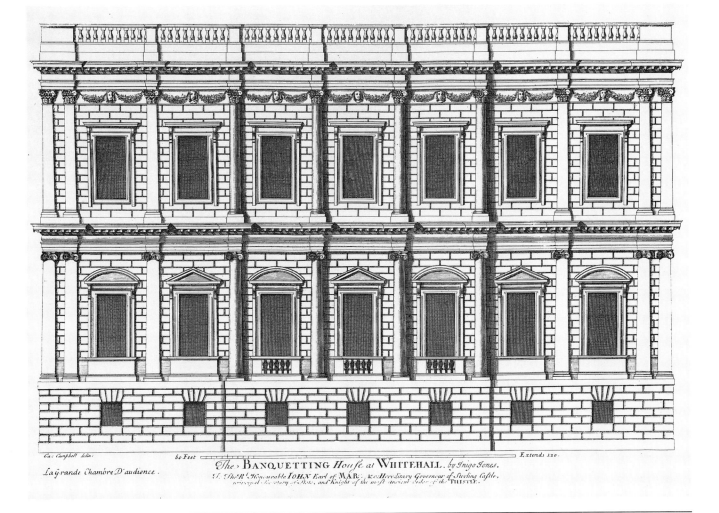

La grande Chambre D'audience.

The BANQUETTING *House at* WHITEHALL. *by Inigo Jones.*

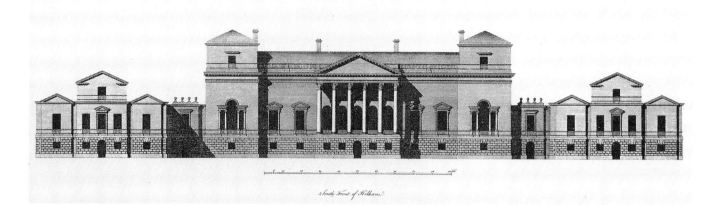

2 South Front of Holkham.

8 Holkham Hall, Norfolk. Begun in 1734 for the Earl of Leicester, to the designs of William Kent. (J Woolfe and J Gandon, *Vitruvius Britannicus*, vi, 1771)

achieved his effects by large statements, emphatically made, each component bearing upon the next in a sweeping, operatic development which culminated at the massively assertive portico set in front of the towering entrance hall. This, appropriately for the gift of a grateful nation to the victorious Duke of Marlborough, is a martial architecture; an architecture of visceral excitement which can stand comparison with the best of the European baroque. William Kent's Holkham, begun only ten years after Blenheim was completed, uses the classical language entirely differently. It is composed of a series of discrete elements, each one of which could stand alone and retain its identity. The portico is a point of balance rather than a climax. The composition achieves its success by subtle variations in the plane of the façade, delimiting the individual units which are tied together by an overall system of proportions and ratios.

If Blenheim is kinetic grand opera, then Holkham is static chamber music of a form too subtle and learned for any but architects of the highest quality. Herein lay the contradiction at the heart of the national style: it could be built satisfactorily but not especially well by those of 'ordinary Capacities' at whom the pattern books were aimed. The first Palladian architects in England, Jones and Webb, and the best of the eighteenth-century Palladian revival architects, the neo-Palladians, grasped the

essential difficulty which is involved in achieving the simple, and it is testimony to the difficulty that even the best sometimes failed. Later Palladianism too easily became palely imitative and too reliant upon the essentially pictorial, received forms.

Vitruvius Britannicus was a celebration of British architecture; the third volume, published in 1725, was very specifically a celebration of the neo-Palladian country house, particularly as designed by Colen Campbell. It included illustrations of all his most important, seminal works: the great houses, Wanstead and Houghton [**10,11**]; and the villas, Mereworth, Stourhead and Newby. Despite the hopes which Lord Shaftesbury had expressed for 'our Prince's Palace and our House of Parliament', the national style was first and foremost the country house style. In the eighteenth century, it has been noted, country house building 'provided the field in which architectural styles competed, played themselves out, or evolved'.[18] However, whilst the country provided the field for building activity, it was the city which provided the establishment structure at the Office of Works which brought neo-Palladian architects into the positions of prominence which invited further patronage.

Throughout the seventeenth and eighteenth centuries the Office of Works was at the heart of the architectural establishment, providing academic and practical training, a continuity of practice, and

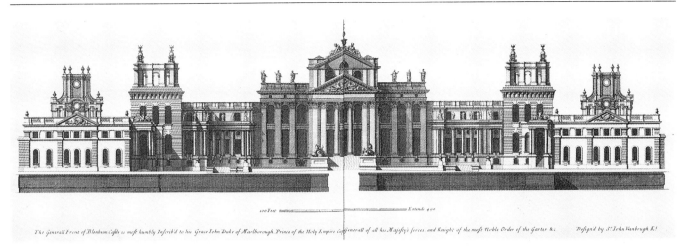

The Generall Front of Blenheim Castle is most humbly Inscrib'd to his Grace Iohn Duke of Marlborough, Prince of the Holy Empire Captiongenerall of all his Majesty's forces and Knight of the most Noble Order of the Garter &c.   Design'd by S:r Iohn Vanbrugh K:t

paid posts.[19] With the death in 1726 of the Comptroller of the King's Works, Sir John Vanbrugh, the last of the old guard of officers appointed under the Surveyor-General, Sir Christopher Wren, the way was clear for a Palladian take-over. In fact, the neo-Palladians had already made inroads into the establishment. William Benson, the builder of Wilbury, had engineered the dismissal of Wren from the Surveyorship in 1718 and had himself appointed in his place, with Colen Campbell as his Deputy. The unscrupulous Benson, according to Nicholas Hawksmoor, 'got more in one year (for confounding the King's Works) than Sr. Chris. Wren did in 40 years for his honest endeavours'. However, he

overreached himself and was forced to resign in 1719, taking Campbell with him, after being caught out in his scheme to rebuild the Houses of Parliament by falsely insisting that the existing building was in danger of collapse.[20]

Benson was succeeded as Surveyor by the Whig country gentleman and amateur architect, Sir Thomas Hewett, who appointed Westby Gill as his Deputy and perhaps was responsible for appointing Nicholas Dubois, the translator of Leoni's edition of Palladio, as Master Mason. Hewett died in 1726 and was succeeded by another political appointee, Richard Arundell, a Yorkshire landowner who had close connections with both of the 'Architect Earls', Lords Burlington and

9 Blenheim Palace, Oxfordshire. Begun in 1705 by Sir John Vanbrugh for the 1st Duke of Marlborough; work continued until 1716; completed by Nicholas Hawksmoor, 1722–5. (Colen Campbell, *Vitruvius Britannicus*, I, 1715)

10 Wanstead House, Essex. Colen Campbell's second design for this house for Sir Richard Child; demolished 1824. (*Vitruvius Britannicus*, I, 1715)

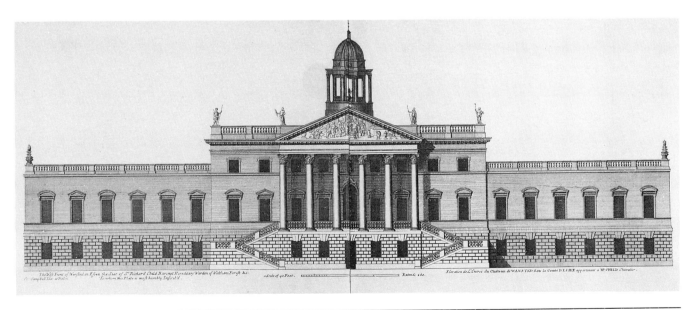

The West Front of Wanstead in Essex, the Seat of S:r Richard Child Baronet Hereditary Warden of Waltham Forest &c.   a Scale of 40 Feet.   Extends 260.   Elevation de L'Entrée du Chateau de WANSTED dans le Comté D'ESSEX appartenant a M:r CHILD Chevalier.
C. Campbell Inv. et Delin.   To whom this Plate is most humbly Inscrib'd.

Pembroke. It was to Burlington that he owed his seat in Parliament as MP for Knaresborough in Yorkshire, and it can be presumed that he would not have been slow to exercise his patronage within the Office of Works in Burlington's favour. In fact, during the course of the eleven years of his Surveyorship, Arundell was able to fill six of the Clerk of Works posts which fell vacant with men of Palladian persuasion, chief among whom were Henry Flitcroft, Burlington's protégé, and Roger Morris, the designer, with Lord Pembroke, of the Palladian Bridge at Wilton. William Kent and Daniel Garrett also owed their advancement in the Works to Burlington's patronage, and two others, Isaac Ware and John Vardy, if they did not owe their initial appointment to office to the influence of Burlington, were certainly indebted to him later in their careers when they worked on the publications which he sponsored.

The position of William Kent, as the one great neo-Palladian architect in office, was of particular importance. He failed to obtain the Comptrollership of the Works in 1726 because First Minister Walpole had reserved it for the considerably lesser Palladian, Thomas Ripley, who had supervised the building of Walpole's house, Houghton Hall, designed by Campbell. Kent's compensation was to be given the post of Master Carpenter. Following the death of Dubois in 1735, Kent was appointed by his fellow Yorkshireman, Arundell, to the post of Master Mason, and he was also granted the Deputy Surveyorship. In these various official capacities it was Kent who was able to determine the style of the standard-setting official buildings of the 1730s and 1740s, the Royal Mews at Charing Cross, the Treasury Buildings and the Horse Guards in Whitehall and the Queen's Library at St James's. He also emulated his Palladian predecessors, Jones and Webb, by producing an unbuilt project for a royal palace and further, perhaps attempting to satisfy the spirit of Lord Shaftesbury, produced

Elevation of the North front of Houghton in Norfolk the Seat of the Right Honourable Robert Walpole Esqr Chancellor of Exq.^r and
first Lord Com.^r of his Majesty's Treasury.&c: Erected Anno 1723. designed by Colen Campbell Esqr

a Scale of 80 feet
5   10   20   30   40   50   60   70   80   *Extends 166*

Burlingtonian schemes for the rebuilding of the Houses of Parliament.

With a man such as Kent in a position of authority, it mattered little that Burlington had resigned his posts at Court in 1733 with a consequent loss of influence. Before he retired, Burlington had succeeded in laying the foundations for the Palladian take-over of official, metropolitan architecture and, by extension, provincial and country house architecture as well. The Office of Works staff, 'secure in their posts and confirmed in their adherence to Palladian principles . . . were architects not only to George II, but to half the aristocracy of England as well'.[21]

By the 1730s the national style had arrived, established in both town and country. We are concerned here with the style in its early manifestations, but it should be noted, almost as an historical truism, that like all national and international styles, in its very establishment it carried the seeds of its own decay, for style alone cannot sustain great architecture. Robert Venturi, in discussing architectural complexity, uses the example of the Doric temple. His remarks are applicable equally to the English Palladian house:

> The Doric temple's simplicity to the eye is achieved through the famous subtleties and precision of its distorted geometry and the contradictions and tensions inherent in its order. The Doric temple could achieve apparent simplicity through real complexity. When complexity disappeared, as in the late temples, blandness replaced simplicity.[22]

REGINA VIRTUS

THE FOUR BOOKS
OF
ANDREA PALLADIO's
ARCHITECTURE:
WHEREIN,
After a short Treatise of the Five ORDERS,
Those Observations that are most necessary in
BUILDING,
PRIVATE HOUSES, STREETS, BRIDGES, PIAZZAS,
XISTI, and TEMPLES are treated of.

LONDON,
Published by
ISAAC WARE,
Anno MDCCXXXVIII.

12 *The Four Books of*
Andrea Palladio's Architecture
title page of Isaac Ware's
edition, 1738 (*see* p 8)

Wiltshire Palladianism

Wiltshire is a county which is remarkable for its concentration of Palladian endeavour by architects of national importance. In their stylistic context, the Inigo Jones/Isaac de Caus/John Webb Wilton, Webb's Amesbury and William Benson's Wilbury are of particular significance: the first two as examples of the initial period of English Palladianism in the seventeenth century, and the last as the most important house in the opening phase of the eighteenth-century Palladian revival, built nearby in emulation of both the style and the names of its precursors.

We are concerned here with issues of architectural style, influence and patronage, but before giving further consideration to these matters, it must be acknowledged that in one particular area, that of function, a close comparison of the houses is potentially misleading, and a distinction must be drawn.

Wilton, in both size and purpose, is a great country house. Amesbury and its derivative, Wilbury, may be classed as villas. The proliferation of the villa, a type which had been exemplifed in the mid seventeenth century by John Webb's Gunnersbury House in Middlesex, was one of the most significant developments in the history of English architecture.

Throughout the country in the early decades of the eighteenth century, small and medium-sized houses sprang up, broadly in response to one of three needs: to provide a secondary seat for the owner of a great country house; to enable gentlemen to 'retire from the hurries of business, and from getting money, to draw their breath in a clear air';[1] or to satisfy the need for a small, manageable house which was felt by 'country gentlemen of moderate fortune'.[2]

More than most functional types, the villa has tended to become associated with one particular architectural style, the Palladian, and Palladio's *Quattro Libri* provided a wide range of models. The English villa, however, was distinct from its Italian prototype in tending to be sited in scenic grounds, rather than being the focal point of a working farm. In being more often a place of retreat, or of occasional or modest occupation, than the hub of a great estate, the villa was functionally distinct from the country house. It could be smaller in size and more compact in plan, because it did not need to maintain the firm, hierarchical distinctions between the classes of occupant which were inevitable requirements in a large house, fully occupied by family and retainers, and which equally inevitably taxed the inventiveness of all but the most resourceful of architects. It is surely significant that as soon as Amesbury and Wilbury came into permanent family occupation, their accommodation was found wanting and considerable extensions were put in hand.

As extensive service accommodation was not a requirement, it was possible for the villa to be rather more self-contained than the traditional country house with its extensive, subsidiary buildings. The kitchen and related services could be accommodated in the basement rather than in an attached wing, with the main rooms of the house at a raised ground-floor or *piano nobile* level, often reached

by steps up to a portico. The main difference in planning between the English and the Venetian villa, except in cases of extreme fidelity to Italian sources, was the English retention of the grand staircase, which was regarded as a showpiece as much as a mere route between floors.

Wilton was justly celebrated for its architecture, its gardens and its collections.[3] Architecturally, it was a house which had evolved according to circumstance and fashion, rather than being an indivisible, self-contained masterpiece, and it was precisely because it was an harmonious amalgamation of abstractable

13 Holkham Hall, Norfolk: an aerial view showing the pyramidal roofs of the four corner towers

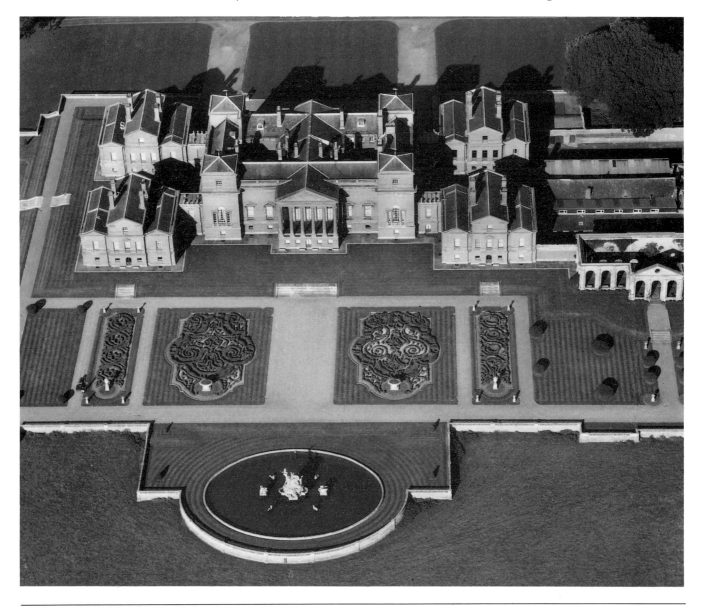

parts that the neo-Palladians found it to be such a rich source of architectural elements, which were perceived to be Jonesian. Both Holkham and Houghton [13, 14], the great neo-Palladian mansions in north Norfolk, were indebted to Wilton for their massing and their corner towers, and the towers, generally with pyramidal roofs, recur in designs throughout the eighteenth century.[4]

The three-light Venetian window, a version of which provided the centrepiece of the Wilton façade, was used occasionally by the architects of the baroque in the late seventeenth and early eighteenth centuries, but following the example of Wilton and Inigo Jones's earlier Queen's Chapel at St James's, it became one of the most commonly used of the neo-Palladians' architectural motifs. The cube room also, introduced to England by Jones, and essayed by John Webb in his unbuilt designs for the Earl of Pembroke's Durham House in the Strand and the Duke of Rutland's Belvoir Castle, proved after Wilton to be an enduring feature of the Palladian house.

The designs of Wilton, Amesbury and Wilbury all achieved a wide circulation in the eighteenth century through their

14 Houghton Hall, Norfolk. The Wilton-style pedimented gables which had been proposed for the corner towers by Campbell were replaced by domes designed by James Gibbs

15   Hinton House, Hinton St George, Somerset: the seventeenth-century south front, built for the Poulett family

16   Brympton d'Evercy, Somerset: the seventeenth-century south front, built for Sir John Posthumous Sydenham, who married a Poulett of Hinton St George

publication in Colen Campbell's *Vitruvius Britannicus*, which brought them to the notice of architects and patrons all over the country. But it is worth considering the extent to which Wilton might have been influential locally, that is, in the south-west of the country, in the mid seventeenth century, prior to its wider publication and the advent of fashionable neo-Palladianism.

A review of the evidence suggests at first sight that, during the middle years of the seventeenth century, pure classical architecture in the innovative and sophisticated manner of Inigo Jones was conspicuous by its absence in both the country and the metropolis. Jones's purely Italianate Queen's House did not inspire a host of imitations in the years after its completion, and nor did Wilton. Three large, copiously pedimented, seventeenth-century houses in nearby Somerset, Hinton House, Brympton d'Evercy and Ashton Court [**15–17**], have all been attributed in the past to Jones or his associates, but their attractive classicism is essentially provincial rather than Jonesian, although in the case of Ashton Court, it is a precocious classicism for the 1630s. The nearest parallel with Wilton which these houses provide is structural rather than stylistic. At Brympton d'Evercy, as at Wilton, the south wall of an earlier house was rebuilt further south to accommodate a new suite of state rooms.[5]

A greater fidelity to the Court style might be expected from Isaac de Caus who, in 1638, during the period of his employment at Wilton, prepared a drawing for the Earl of Cork's Stalbridge in Dorset. The house was demolished in 1822, without adequate record. A surviving illustration shows two classical porches on a Jacobean house, but the exterior betrays no other evidence of a classicising hand.[6] Elsewhere in Dorset, the gabled, artisan mannerist style, customarily interpreted as an early seventeenth-century alternative to Jonesian classicism, appears in a splendid example at Hamworthy [**18**], the Manor

House, the seat of the Carew family, which is now known as the Old Rectory.[7]

There are, however, two houses in Dorset which display an advanced classicism for their date, and which might have been influenced by the innovative example of Wilton: Cranborne Manor House and St Giles's House, Wimborne[19, 20]. Repairs and additions, including the designing of a new west wing, were made at Cranborne, a former royal hunting lodge, by Captain Richard Ryder during the period 1647–50.[8] The house offers a striking parallel with Wilton, for earlier in the seventeenth century an extra storey was added to an existing tower, and a matching tower was built at the other end of the south façade. Capped by pyramidal roofs, these are very like the pre-fire towers at Wilton. The parallel certainly will not have been lost on Ryder, for as master carpenter on the Wilton works during John Webb's post-fire refitting, he surely was closely familiar with that house and with the Jones/Webb style.

It is possible that Ryder was responsible also for the work begun at St Giles's House by Sir Anthony Ashley Cooper, later the 1st Earl of Shaftesbury, in 1651.[9] Here, a well-proportioned, seven-bay, east range was added to older buildings in a restrained manner which distinguishes the house from most of its contemporaries. Although no architect so far has been identified for St Giles's, it is very likely that it will prove to be by someone with either Court or Wilton connections. Given the existence inside the new range of a chimney-piece and ceiling which are both robustly Jonesian in manner, the presence of John Webb at one remove is again not unlikely.[10]

By the eighteenth century, the classical style was firmly established, and with the benefit of more surviving documentation, the activities of architects, the charting of influences and the evidence of cross-fertilization is altogether clearer.

In Wiltshire, the second generation neo-Palladian, Henry Flitcroft, was involved in work at Amesbury (and also,

17 Ashton Court, Long Ashton, Avon (formerly Somerset): the south-west wing of *c.* 1635, built for Sir Thomas Smyth MP

18 Manor House, Hamworthy, Poole, Dorset, now the Rectory, built *c.* 1650 for the Carew family

19 Cranborne Manor
House, Cranborne, Dorset:
the new west wing of
1647–50. The house was
acquired by Sir Robert Cecil,
1st Earl of Salisbury, early in
the seventeenth century

20 St Giles's House,
Wimborne St Giles, Dorset:
the mid seventeenth-century
east range

in the period 1740 – 4 at St Giles's House, Wimborne), and his contemporary, Roger Morris, collaborated with the 9th Earl of Pembroke in designing the Palladian Bridge at Wilton. Morris has also been suggested as the architect of the neo-Palladian remodelling of Lydiard Park, a house which has elements in common with Wilton. Lord Pembroke's taste for the architecture of the Veneto, indulged during his Grand Tour, was probably stimulated during his period at Christ Church, Oxford, where he was studying at the time of the construction of Dean Aldrich's proto-Palladian Peckwater Quadrangle, towards which he contributed £20.[11]

The better known 'Architect Earl', Lord Burlington, is represented in Wiltshire by Tottenham Park, which drew on both Wilton and Amesbury; and Colen Campbell by the prototypical eighteenth-century villa, Stourhead, which he designed for Henry Hoare, the banker. Flitcroft again was involved at both these houses, as executant architect at Tottenham, and as the designer of garden buildings at Stourhead. Benson also might have been involved at Stourhead: Hoare was his brother-in-law. Certainly the two men collaborated on building a new chancel for the parish church at Quarley [**21**], a Hoare property which was situated just over the county boundary in Hampshire. The Venetian window in the east end, a curiously sophisticated creation in its small, village church setting, is inscribed: 'GULIELMUS BENSON & HENRICUS HOARE ARM: F.A.D. 1723'.[12] The inscription appears on the inside as well, with the names reversed. The side lights of the three-light window have been filled in.

Lord Burlington's central role in the neo-Palladian take-over of the Office of Works in the early eighteenth century has been noted. These Wiltshire houses demonstrate one of the ways in which that take-over was extended to country-house architecture, through the network of familial and professional relationships which existed between patrons and architects. Burlington was a cousin of the Duke of Queensberry: the employment of his protégé, Flitcroft, followed at Amesbury. Lord Bruce of Tottenham Park was Burlington's brother-in-law: Burlington designed his house and employed Flitcroft to carry out his ideas. Henry Hoare was Burlington's banker[13] and he employed Colen Campbell, who had been working on the remodelling of Burlington House, Piccadilly, to design Stourhead, where Flitcroft also was to be employed. Hoare was, furthermore, a relative of William Benson of Wilbury, who was himself associated professionally with Campbell. In addition to the remodelling of Burlington House, Campbell designed the London house of Lord Pembroke, Pembroke House, Whitehall.

The differences in the interpretation and adaptation of Italian and Jonesian models, which are shown in the work of the Architect Earls, have been discussed by James Lees-Milne.[14] However, notwithstanding the variations in neo-Palladian form which are manifested in their buildings, the two men clearly had a community of interest. This perhaps was encouraged through their mutual friendship with Sir Andrew Fountaine. In his *Essay in Defence of Ancient Architecture*, published in 1728, Robert Morris stressed the debt which future ages would owe to Burlington, Pembroke and Fountaine, as the principal practitioners of ancient architecture and the preservers of antiquity. Sir Andrew was a less notable architect than either Burlington or Pembroke, but as 'one of the keenest virtuosi in Europe',[15] and the honorary cataloguer and custodian of the Wilton collections, the encomium was just. He enjoyed the friendship and confidence of both the 8th and 9th Earls of Pembroke, and Burlington's own high regard for him was made clear by his gift of the Pellegrini paintings, removed from Burlington House during its remodelling, which now adorn Sir Andrew's Norfolk seat, Narford Hall.[16]

21 St Michael, Quarley, Hampshire: the Venetian (east) window, installed by William Benson and Henry Hoare in 1723

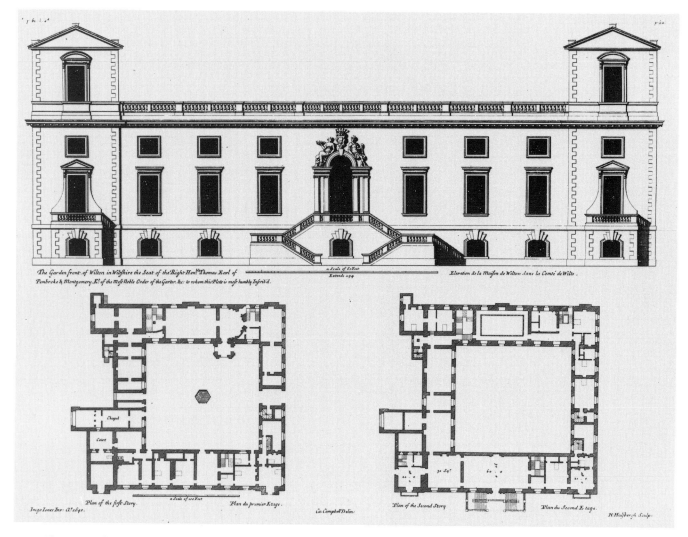

The Garden front of Wilton in Wilshire the Seat of the Right Hon.ble Thomas Earl of
Pembroke & Montgomery, K.t of the Most Noble Order of the Garter, &c: to whom this Plate is most humbly Inscrib'd.

a Scale of 60 Feet
Extends 194

Elevation de la Maison de Wilton dans le Comté de Wilts.

Chapel
Court

Plan of the first Story   a Scale of 100 Feet   Plan du premier Etage.

Plan of the Second Story   Plan du Second Etage.

Imgo Iones Inv: A° 1640.   Ca: Campbell Delin: H.Hulsbergh Sculp:

22 Elevation of south front
and plans of ground and
first floors. (Colen Campbell,
Vitruvius Britannicus, ii,
1717)

Wilton House

Ownership and Outline History

A 'priory of nuns' existed on the site of Wilton House in the tenth century.[1] It was succeeded by a Benedictine abbey in the thirteenth century, which survived until the Abbess, Cecilia Bodenham, surrendered the possessions to the Crown at the Dissolution.[2]

The abbey buildings and estates were granted in various stages between 1542 and 1544 to William Herbert, son of Richard, Gentleman Usher to Henry VII. By his marriage in c. 1534 to Ann Parr he had become brother-in-law to Catherine, who married Henry VIII in 1543. Herbert stood high in royal favour and was knighted during the same year. He was subsequently made a Knight of the Garter in 1548, and on successive days in October 1551 was elevated to the peerage as Baron Herbert of Cardiff and created Earl of Pembroke, thus becoming one of the most powerful noblemen of the time.

Expenditure on building works at Wilton began in 1543,[3] and over the next twenty years a major programme of rebuilding was implemented. At the time of a survey made of the 1st Earl's lands c. 1565, it was reported that he had newly constructed all the houses, gardens, orchards and other appurtenances at a cost of more than £10,000.[4]

Elizabeth I passed three nights at this rebuilt house in 1574 as the guest of William's son Henry, 2nd Earl of Pembroke, 'during all which tyme her majesty was boeth merry and pleasant'.[5] Further royal visits were made by James I and his Queen, and by Charles I who, as John Aubrey tells us, 'did love Wilton above all places: and came thither every Sommer'.[6] According to Aubrey, Philip, the 4th Earl, was following a suggestion of Charles when he embarked upon the alteration and enlargement of Wilton House and the laying out of the garden in the 1630s, the works being carried out under the direction of Isaac de Caus, with the detailed advice of Inigo Jones, who was in turn assisted by John Webb.

It has been suggested that family and financial misfortune had some bearing on the progress of this rebuilding scheme: the palatial design by de Caus was begun, but eventually completed in a reduced form. In 1635, on the death of his eldest son Charles, who had been married the previous year, the Earl forfeited his daughter-in-law's dowry of £25,000, which had to be returned. His later estrangement from his wife the Countess, Lady Anne Clifford, resulted in a further financial loss, with the removal from Wilton of her personal income.[7]

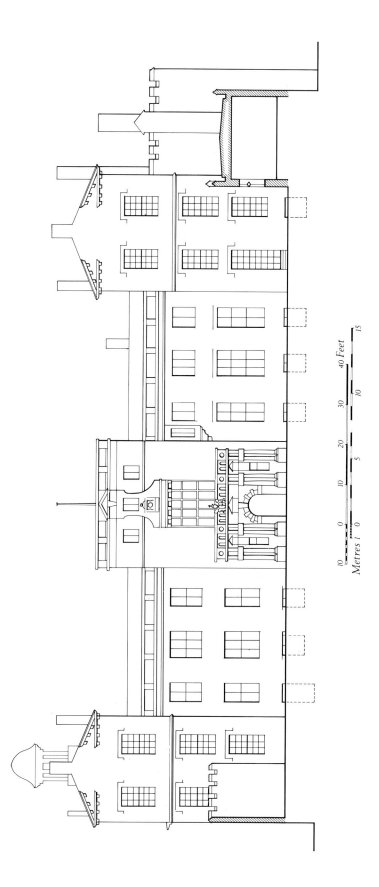

23a North elevation: the present entrance front, showing the forecourt raised by James Wyatt

Metres 1 0

10   0   10   20   30   40 Feet

0   5   10   15

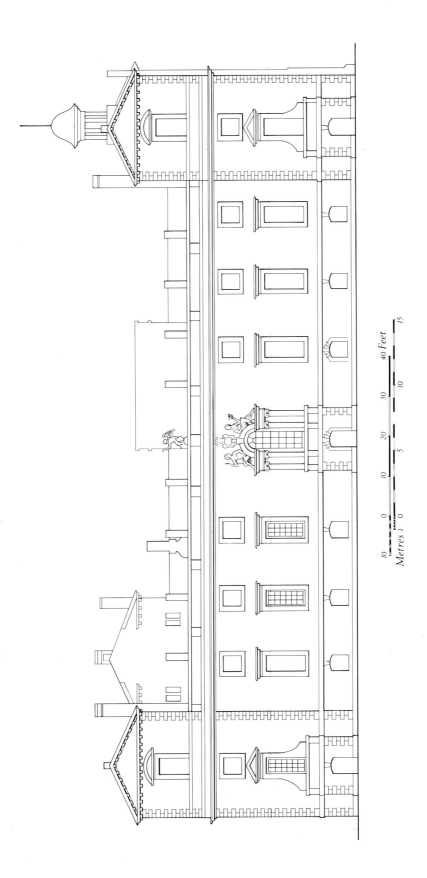

23b South elevation: the garden front

Metres 1 0   5   10
                    0   10   20   30   40 *Feet*
10   15

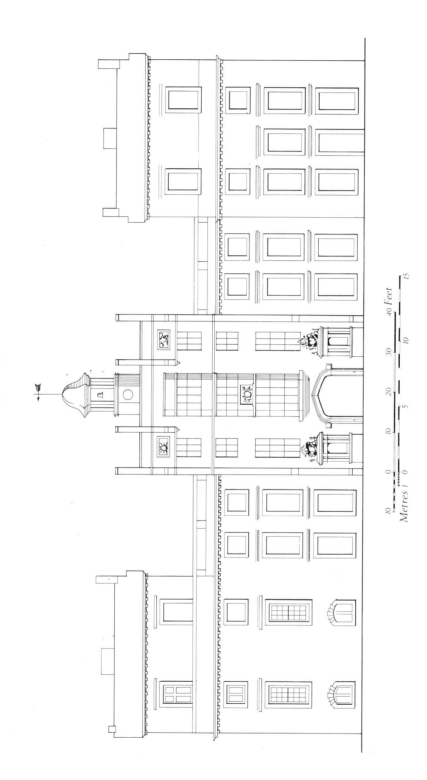

23c East elevation: the former entrance front

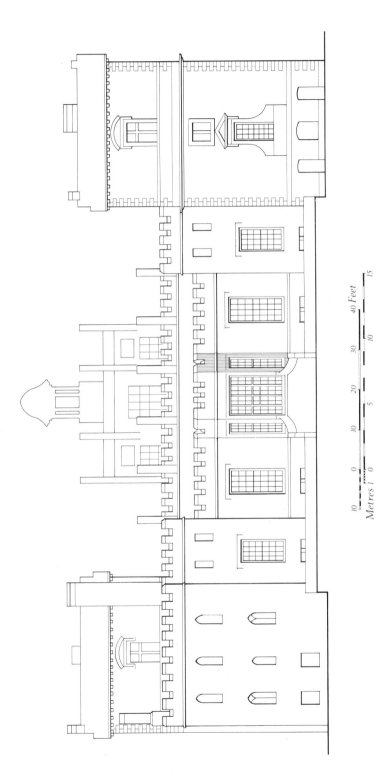

23d West elevation: the front overlooking the Italian garden

However critical these financial problems might have been, they certainly do not appear to have presented Pembroke with long-term difficulties, for in 1641 he was able to take over Durham House in the Strand and contemplate a grandiloquent rebuilding scheme by John Webb. This design remained on paper and Webb prepared a smaller design in 1649, also 'not taken'.[8] By this time the architect was fully engaged upon further extensive works at Wilton, where a fire in the new south range in 1647 prompted the remodelling upon which rests the house's fame as the pre-eminent monument of English Palladianism. Another fire in 1705, this time in the north range, caused further considerable damage which necessitated the remodelling recorded in the plan [22] published by Colen Campbell in 1717.[9]

During the course of the eighteenth century, the architectural ambitions of the Earls of Pembroke, especially of the 9th and 10th Earls, appear to have been fulfilled largely in the erection of buildings in the grounds, important contributions being made by Roger Morris and by Sir William Chambers. This emphasis was drastically altered by George, the 11th Earl who, between 1801 and 1812, entrusted a major programme of alterations to James Wyatt, which in the words of the architect's recent biographer represented 'an unfortunate attempt to transform the most important seventeenth-century classical house into a medieval abbey'.[10] Wyatt's new gothic entrance front was rebuilt in 1914 but much of his work survives [23, 24].

Wilton House remains the seat of the Earls of Pembroke.

24 Aerial view from above the north forecourt. (Photographed by Traffic Technology Ltd, Warminster, 1983)

The Sixteenth-Century House

Evidence is sparse for even a tentative reconstruction of the abbey at Wilton prior to the Dissolution. William Worcestre measured the abbey church in 1478 by means of his 'steps',[11] but the first description of the house was not made until 1603, when Sir Roger Wilbraham visited and found: 'a faire howse called Wilton, a large & high built square of hewen stone: the roomes having ther lightes but one way into the square one malencholic & dark'.[12] We might conjecture that the quadrangular house so described was not a completely new structure of *c*. 1550, but incorporated parts of the abbey. A similar conversion of ex-monastic buildings was taking place at nearby Lacock, where similar early Renaissance detailing occurs.

Eighteenth-century plans of Wilton [79a, 80a see pp 62, 64] depict massively thick walls on the ground and first floors at the southern end of the west range, and in the position of the north-west corner tower. These would be inexplicable in a house which had been newly built in the 1550s, and investigation of the present structure shows that much of the stonework in the outer north and east walls and in the courtyard walls is certainly re-used. There is also, low down at the south end of the east façade, a blocked, semicircular archway which is possibly of twelfth-century origin. Evidence elsewhere of an earlier structure was revealed during the investigation of dry rot in 1948, when a chamfered window opening was found behind the panelling in the north-east corner of the Single Cube Room, and a door was found at ground level at the same corner [25]. A large, blocked window in the north wall of the adjacent Double Cube Room was also uncovered, raising the question of whether this might originally have lit a first-floor refectory over an undercroft.[13] The south side 'roomes & Lodgeings' were described in 1635 as being built upon 'archt Cellars', suggestive of such an undercroft.[14] Recent

25 Single Cube Room: door inserted at north-east corner into the cloister, showing chamfered jamb of medieval window

investigation within the courtyard cloister roofs has revealed the existence of window cornices for blocked mullion and transom windows. These can be seen with later windows on the Buckler drawing of 1803 which shows the Holbein porch *in situ*.[15] This underlines the justness of Wilbraham's remark concerning the lighting of the rooms from the inner court only, and offers further confirmation of the degree to which the sixteenth-century house was a remodelling of an earlier building. It would be surprising indeed if a newly built house of the mid sixteenth century, belonging to a powerful courtier, had not had windows looking fashionably outwards, and we know enough about Pembroke's house to recognise that it was characterised by a degree of architectural ambition.

The new gatehouse and east entrance range which Pembroke built were illustrated on the survey of his lands made *c*. 1565 [26]. The design was roughly contemporary with Protector Somerset's Somerset House in the Strand,[16] and whilst Wilton's front was not of the same order of sophistication, the pedimented gables over the central entrance tower and over the lower wings to each side,

26 Gatehouse and east entrance range, illustrated in the *Survey of the Lands of William, 1st Earl of Pembroke* (*c.* 1565) (WRO, 2057/S3)

27 The east front: comparative drawings of the sixteenth century **a** and present façades **b**

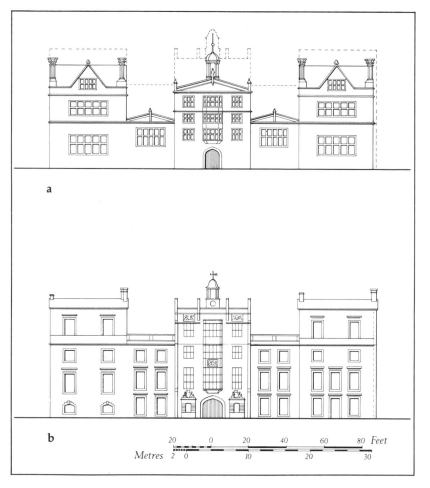

which linked the centre with the end towers, had a comparable air of early Renaissance endeavour [**27**]. The ornate lead downpipes, which are shown on the survey drawing, provide additional evidence of the stylistically advanced qualities of Pembroke's house; further examples survive on the courtyard side of the east range, where they harmonise well with a sixteenth-century gadrooned string course [**28, 29**].

The major survival from the Tudor house, the so-called 'Holbein Porch', is yet more remarkably sophisticated for its date, demonstrating an unusual understanding for the proportions and relationships of its superimposed Orders. It originally provided the entrance from the courtyard to the north range of the house which contained the Great Hall. Being positioned off-centre to give access to a screens passage, it ran the risk of being demolished in a later age more inclined to symmetry, but Inigo Jones's opinion related by Aubrey that the porch [**30**] was 'as good architecture as any was in England' ensured its preservation *in situ*.[17] It was resited eventually in the gardens following its removal to make way for Wyatt's cloisters. The traditional attribution of the design of the porch to Holbein appears to have begun with Aubrey, but it can be discounted as the artist died in 1543, some years before it was built. Its richly carved heraldic panels, displaying the arms of Herbert encircled by the Garter, date these features at the earliest to 1548, the year the honour was conferred.

The 1st Earl's house was visited in 1635 by Lieutenant Hammond and described by him at some length. First he visited the gallery, 'richly hung and adorn'd with stately and faire pictures', then passing through a withdrawing room and the Earl's bedchamber he came to the King's chamber, 'the hangings therein being Cloth of Gold, and on over the Chimney Peece is the statue of King Henry 8th richly cut and gilded over'. Next he passed through the King's withdrawing room, the billiard room and the chapel before reaching the great dining chamber where he saw 'a most curious Chimney Peece, of Alabaster, Touch-Stone and Marble, cut with severall statues, the Kings and his Lordships owne Armes richly set out'. Lastly he 'march'd downe through the fayre Great Hall, and stately 4 square built Court, beautify'd about, with the Kings and his owne Armes, by the archt Cellers into the Gardens', where he found a great variety of new works in progress including a 'rare Water-worke now making . . . the finishing which . . . peece of Skill . . . will cost (they say) a great Summe of Money'.[18] (*See* p 82 for a description of the gardens.)

Hammond was thus the first person to record his impressions of the new work begun in the garden for the 4th Earl. Work on the south front commenced soon afterwards.

The Seventeenth-Century House

The genesis of the building works of the 1630s at Wilton is well known. Aubrey relates that it was Charles I

> 'that did put Philip . . . Earle of Pembroke upon making this magnificent garden and grotto, and to build that side of the house that fronts the garden, with two stately pavilions at each end, all *al Italiano*. His Majesty intended to have had it all designed by his own architect, Mr Inigo Jones, who being at that time, about 1633, engaged in his Majesties buildings at Greenwich, could not attend to it; but he recommended it to an ingeniouse architect, Monsieur Solomon de Caus, a Gascoigne, who performed it very well; but not without the advice and approbation of Mr Jones'.[19]

Inigo Jones is known to have visited Wilton during the time of the 3rd Earl, a personal friend, most memorably in 1620 when he was summoned there by Pembroke and James I to carry out his investigation into the origins of Stonehenge.[20] The recommendation of Jones, as Surveyor to the Crown and as a man familiar with the house, was a natural one for the King to make. It was equally

28 Detail of downpipe shown in **29**

29 The courtyard side of the east range entrance tower, seen from the roof of the south range

30 John Buckler's drawing of the Holbein Porch *in situ*, 1803. (WAS, Devizes)

to be expected, given the tremendous amount of official work which he had to do, that Jones, whilst retaining an interest, should pass the commission on to another. In his seminal article, 'The South Front of Wilton House', Howard Colvin demonstrated that the other was not Solomon de Caus but his son or nephew, Isaac, who had already worked with Jones at the Whitehall Banqueting House, and who in 1633–4 was acting as the Surveyor's executant architect at Covent Garden.[21]

Surviving account books show that work on the garden at Wilton began in 1632–3, with a high point of expenditure in 1634–5.[22] Work on the house does not appear to have begun until 1636 when de Caus was instructed to 'take downe . . . that side of Wilton house which is towards the Garden & such other parts as shall bee necessary & rebuild it anew with additions according to ye Plott which is agreed'. Mr Brookes, the housekeeper, was required to remove 'all the stuffe in ye roomes & Lodgeings of that side of the house which is to bee pulled downe & rebuilt'.[23]

The garden executed and later published [31] by de Caus was symmetrically placed to the south of the proposed new range.[24] The appearance of this range is preserved for us in a drawing first published by Colvin [33], which shows a front nearly four hundred feet in length, with a central hexastyle pedimented portico aligned with the central avenue of the garden.[25]

Lieutenant Hammond referred to sixteenth-century Wilton as 'stately and Princelike', although the 1st Earl of Pembroke's house could never have matched the prodigious piles erected by some. Sir John Thynne's Longleat, William Cecil's Theobalds, Sir Christopher Hatton's Holdenby and the Earl of Suffolk's Audley End were all to exceed it in size and ambition. All these men must have recognised that the 'one essential condition for retaining their wealth and standing was to continue in royal favour, in office . . . and to do this it was wisdom to entertain and accommodate the court'.[26] Such entertainment had reached its height under Elizabeth and James I, but by the 1630s the times were changing, and Philip, the 4th Earl of Pembroke, was at the end of a tradition in contemplating the building of a house as large as the one proposed by de Caus, which in the width of its façade was unprecedented in English domestic architecture [32]. It was nothing short of palatial, and we must presume that the intention was to place symmetrical suites of apartments for the King and Queen to either side of the central portico. There is no evidence for de Caus's intentions behind this long façade, but the presumption must be that further ranges would have been planned to provide a house built around two courtyards, divided by a central, spinal range positioned behind the portico. Such was the disposition of Durham House in the Strand [34], the aristocratic palace which John Webb proposed for the Earl of Pembroke during the following decade, the façade of which represented a restatement by Webb, in considerably more sophisticated and dramatic terms, of de Caus's grand but uninspired elevation for Wilton.[27]

Wilton, in the manner of large courtier houses, was a tribute to the monarch.

Durham House, conceived during the period of Pembroke's espousal of the Parliamentary cause in the Civil War, was a challenge. We might set both Wilton and Durham alongside the similarly unexecuted Jones and Webb designs for a new royal palace at Whitehall, and question the degree to which the unrealistic aspirations of the King encouraged architectural delusions in the subject. Both men were to be frustrated ultimately by a shortage of money. De Caus's grand scheme for Wilton was begun, but was then drastically reduced, its place taken by the curtailed scheme which substantially survives today.

The Reduced Scheme

A drawing by de Caus [35] in the Burlington–Devonshire Collection[28] shows that, in effect, the initially revised scheme involved taking the east wing of the grand design, placing a further bay with steps up to an entrance door at its west end in place of the pedimented centrepiece, and adding an enlarged achievement of the Herbert arms over the central Venetian window to reinforce its position as a focal point. The elevation follows the grand design in having œil-de-bœuf windows over the end windows of the main storey: further French influence is

31   Isaac de Caus: elevated prospect of the formal garden from the north, engraved and published in de Caus's *Wilton Garden* of *c.* 1654

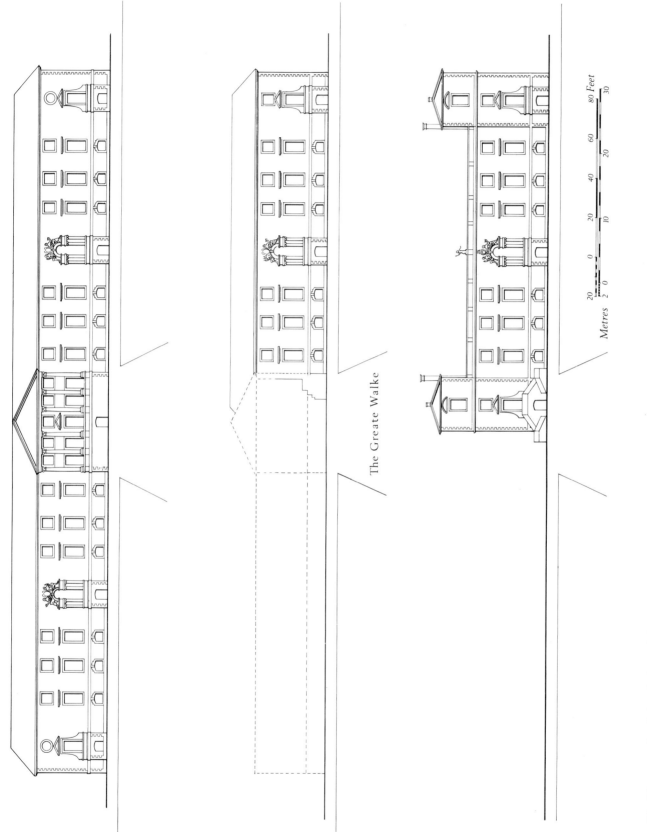

The Greate Walke

Metres 20 2 0

0 20 40 60 80 Feet
2 0 10 20 30

32 The genesis of the design of the south front: the grand scheme, aligned on the central avenue of the garden; the reduced scheme, begun, but altered during building; the towered scheme, as built

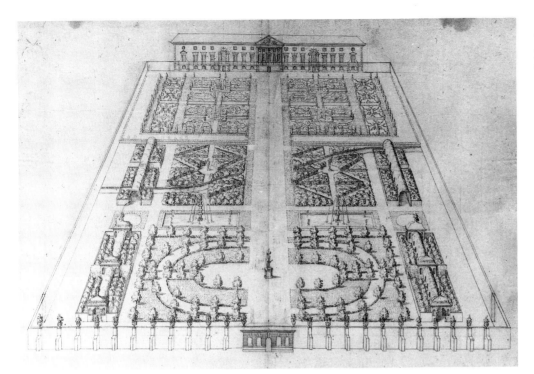

33 Isaac de Caus: view of the garden and the proposed south front. (Worcester College, Oxford)

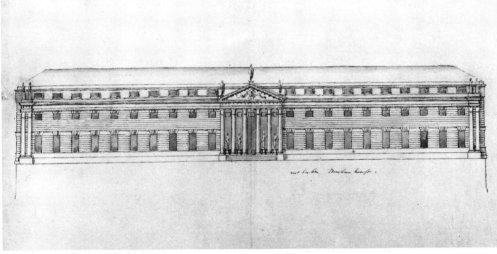

34 John Webb: elevation of the proposed Strand front for the Earl of Pembroke's Durham House, inscribed 'not taken'. (Worcester College, Oxford)

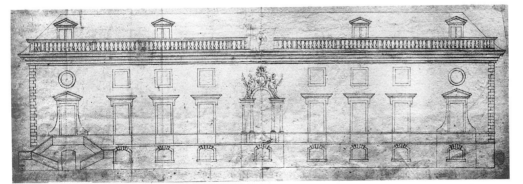

35 Isaac de Caus: the reduced scheme for the south front. (RIBA Drawings Collection)

36 John Buckler's drawing of the south and east fronts, 1804. (WAS, Devizes)

discernible in the dormers of the hipped roof. The features which are mentioned by Aubrey, but not shown by de Caus in his drawing, are the 'two stately pavilions at each end, all *al Italiano*'. These were an afterthought which was dictated not only by the need to provide vertical emphasis to the façade, but was also required by the presence of the Tudor towers at the ends of the east entrance range. To marry satisfactorily the new south wing with the existing range on the east, it was necessary either to demolish the Tudor towers altogether, or rebuild them in a style in keeping with the new south front. The de Caus grand scheme and his drawing for the curtailed scheme (of which there was even a proof engraving)[29] imply the demolition of the Tudor towers. We can perhaps infer from this that the 4th Earl initially intended the new south range, even in its curtailed form, to be merely the first in a total

rebuilding of Wilton, but that the realisation dawned, after work had already begun, that with regard to the entrance front anything more than a remodelling of the original would be beyond his means. It is clear from the existing structure that building activity did take place elsewhere in the house during the seventeenth century, but stress has always rightly been laid upon the towered south front. Prompted by the need to provide strong architectural accents at the ends of both the south and entrance ranges, Wilton's most distinctive and emulated features were created [36].

It is significant that the towers do not project from the plane of the south front [37] in the manner indicated on Colen Campbell's plan. The quoins, which from a distance appear to be marking such a break in the plane of the wall, are merely laid upon the wall surface for purposes of articulation. This sophisticated play with

appearances might be taken as confirmation that the east end tower was
rebuilt after the main lines of the building
had been defined. The subsidence which
it has subsequently undergone as a
consequence of being built on earlier,
perhaps inadequate, foundations further
suggests its status as an afterthought. We
might conclude that the serene south
front of Wilton, the archetype of many of
the great houses of the eighteenth
century, rather than springing fully armed
from the mind of its creator, appears
to have been a design which evolved
piecemeal out of compromise and neces-
sity.

   Notwithstanding its great repute, the
south front is not above criticism, and Sir
William Chambers was one who recognised the compromises which had been
necessary in its making. He found the
centre insufficiently stressed, and the
figures above the Venetian window [**38**]

37   The south front

38   The south front: detail
of centrepiece

'clumsy, ill erected & ill proportioned'. The main-floor windows he considered 'handsom, but ill supported', and the attic windows too close to them, causing the pediments of the tower windows to touch their sills. The balustrade he found 'too high, wretchedly designed & very ill executed'. 'Upon the whole', he concluded, 'the merit of this performance is rather to be sought for in the general form & in the Proportions of the three principal masses, than in the detail'.[30] The towers are crucial for this general effect.

Italian precedents for the design of the towers can be found not only in the work of Palladio,[31] but also more directly in that of his pupil Scamozzi [39].[32] It is perhaps here in particular, in shifting the emphasis of the design of the exterior away from the Francophile, which he had favoured initially, towards the Italianate, that de Caus received some 'advice and approbation' from Jones, who had met the ageing Scamozzi in Venice in 1614. Further light is shed on the original appearance of the Wilton

towers, before their rebuilding after the fire of 1647, by a drawing in the Society of Antiquaries [40] which shows them clearly terminated not by the familiar pedimented gables, but by hipped, tiled roofs of decidedly *al Italiano* form.[33]

It might be conjectured that the towers had a functional as well as an aesthetic purpose beyond that of merely providing accommodation. The handsome straight-headed doors of mid seventeenth-century date [41] which give access from the towers to the roof suggest viewing the garden from the leads as a pastime.[34]

In taking down 'that side of Wilton house which is towards the Garden', de Caus retained the north wall towards the central court, and built the new south wall further south to align with the end of the east front and to produce the width required for the grander rooms which he proposed. The south-facing windows of the new range went some way towards correcting the impression of inadequate lighting recorded by Wilbraham in 1603. De Caus also retained the thick (4'6") wall which marked the west end of the south range of the earlier house. This now separates the Single Cube Room from the Hunting Room. Later, following the abandonment of the grand scheme, he built the new end wall of the west tower about three feet further west than perfect symmetry would dictate, to bring it into closer alignment with the central avenue of the garden. The double staircase at this point, which is shown in seventeenth and early eighteenth-century illustrations, in projecting beyond the line of the end wall, helped to foster an illusion of axial alignment. The staircase had been removed by the mid eighteenth century.

An examination of the structure of the south range confirms that a remodelling of the interior took place not only after the 1647 fire, but also during the original building programme. The brick partition walls at each end of the Double Cube Room are irregularly bonded into the north and south walls. One would certainly expect them to be regularly bonded

39 V Scamozzi: design from *L'Idea della Architettura Universale*, I, III, 1615

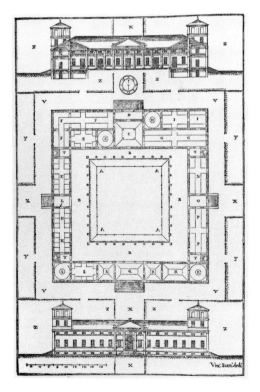

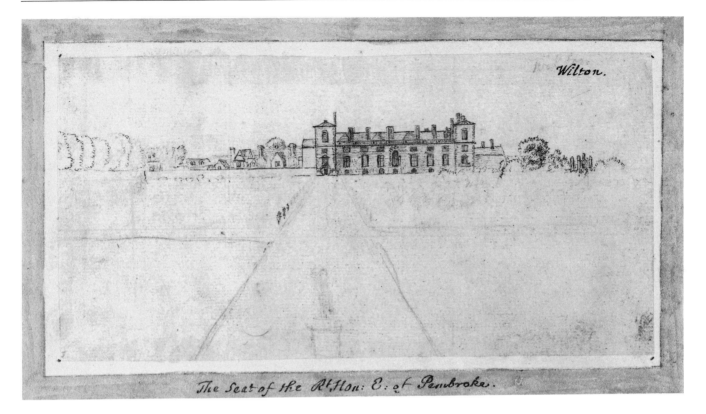

Wilton.

The Seat of the Rt Hon: E: of Pembroke.

into the new south wall at least, and it is suggested therefore that these walls are insertions, and that the reduced building project resulted in a replanning and subdivision within a year or two of 1636. This would go some way towards explaining the internal peculiarities of relationship between window openings and cross walls in this range: the internal symmetry is more apparent than actual. (The rooftop balustrade also is asymmetrically arranged.)

The existence of the Double Cube Room before the fire can be inferred from Aubrey's reminder to himself, in which, after describing the ceiling by de Critz, he adds a 'Quaere' to ask 'Dr Caldicot and Mr Uniades, what was the story or picture in the cieling when the house was burnt'.[35]

The Post-Fire Refitting

The 1647 fire was caused, in the words of Aubrey, 'by airing of the roomes'. In 1648, he goes on, 'Philip . . . re-edifyed it, by the advice of Inigo Jones; but he,

40 The pre-fire south front, with pyramidal roofs on the towers. (Society of Antiquaries, *County Seats*, VII)

41 Door in south-west tower, viewed from roof of south range

being then very old, could not be there in person, but left it to Mr Webb . . .'[36] The fire has been dated towards the end of the year by a reference in the Salisbury Churchwardens' Accounts to mending twenty-five buckets that were split whilst the blaze was being fought.[37] The extent of the fire has been discussed by Colvin, and his conclusions have been supported by recent structural investigation, which confirms that the south range was severely damaged but that the masonry shell survived. Above the coving of the Single and Double Cube Rooms there is clear evidence of internal fire scorching and splashing of molten lead on the upper walls. Further, the existence of blocked windows in the south wall behind the coved ceilings corresponds with the external apertures at this level. These windows, and the surviving fragments of fire-damaged painted wall plaster, indicate that the coving of each of these rooms by Webb replaced previous flat ceilings, with upper tiers of windows within the friezes. The sockets for the joists of the original ceiling are still visible in the roof space above the springing of the coving.

Webb's responsibility for the post-fire refitting is demonstrated not only by drawings, some of which are dated 1649, but also by the accounts published by Colvin which cover the years 1650 and 1651, and show that he was in charge at an annual fee of £40, and that both London and country workmen were employed.[38] One of the craftsmen involved was the master carpenter, Richard Ryder, who had worked with Webb before, and who was in 1647–50 involved in repairs and alterations to Cranborne Manor House.[39] On two occasions he charged for coming over to Cranborne from Wilton. Webb might well have received advice from Ryder, just as we might presume that he himself offered advice on the new work at Cranborne. He might also have received advice from Isaac de Caus, for after his building campaign of the 1630s, the Earl of Pembroke settled a pension on him for life, and provided him with lodgings in the house.[40] In these circumstances, Webb hardly would have needed further advice from the aged Inigo Jones, and indeed it is extremely unlikely that he would have been offered any. By this time the 4th Earl was inclining towards the Parliamentary cause, and the 5th Earl, who succeeded his father in 1650, made his views clear when he referred later to 'Iniquity Jones': His Majesty's Surveyor was clearly *persona non grata*.[41]

Apart from refitting the interior, Webb was responsible for redesigning the upper stages of the towers on the south front, replacing the hipped tile roofs with the pedimented gables which were first recorded in a drawing made in 1669 during the tour of England of Cosimo III, Duke of Tuscany [42].[42] Both the original

42   The south front, drawn by Magalotti in 1669 during the tour of Cosimo III. (B M Add 33767B, fo24)

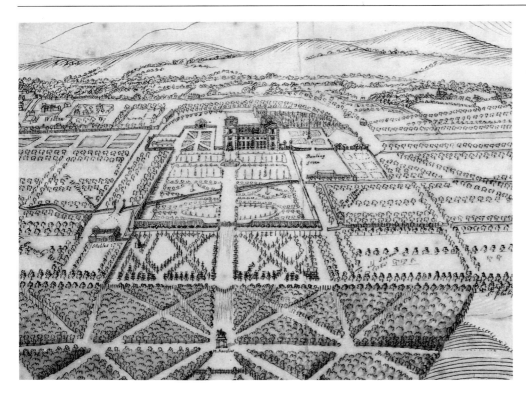

43   Elevated prospect from the south, drawn by William Stukeley, 5 September 1723. (Bodleian Library, Gough Maps 33, 19r)

hipped roof towers on the north side and Webb's reconstructions on the south are illustrated in a painting of *c.* 1700 which is at Wilton. It was probably not until after the fire of 1705 in the north range, that the four towers were once again given the same profile, their pedimented gables being recorded in a drawing made by Stukeley in 1723 [**43**].[43]

By May 1652, Webb's new state apartments were complete: Lodewyk Huygens was conducted around the 'nouvelle bastie a l'Italienne' and he found the ceilings 'tout peint d'une assez bonne main'.[44] In 1654 John Evelyn was equally impressed by the 'Dining-roome in the modern built part towards the Garden, richly gilded, & painted with story by De Creete, also some other apartments, as that of Hunting Landskips by Pierce: some magnificent chimney-pieces, after the French best manner . . .'[45] Some years later Pepys passed by but Lord Pembroke was away so he could not go in. He took comfort in the thought that the house did not promise much anyway, being badly situated in a low valley.[46]

One man's 'low valley' is another man's 'pleasant Vale'; the editor of Defoe's 'Tour' bowed to no one in his admiration for Wilton:

It is universally acknowledged, that the Apartments called the Salon, and the great Dining-room, are the noblest Pieces of Architecture, that have been hitherto produced: the first is a Cube of 30 Feet; the other is a double Cube of 60 by 30; and both of them 30 Feet high. When you are entered these grand Apartments, such Variety strikes upon you every Way, that you scarce know to which Hand to turn yourself first.[47]

In a letter of 6 April 1655 to Sir Justinian Isham of Lamport, John Webb advised his employer to have his statues for niches cast from 'Antique moulds' for 'French fashions are you know fantasticall'.[48] Webb, following Jones, was pleased to observe due decorum in design, and whilst the French could not be relied upon for statuary, their 'fantasticall' fashions were entirely appropriate for the more exuberant features of interior decoration: ceilings and chimney-pieces. Webb was a frequent borrower

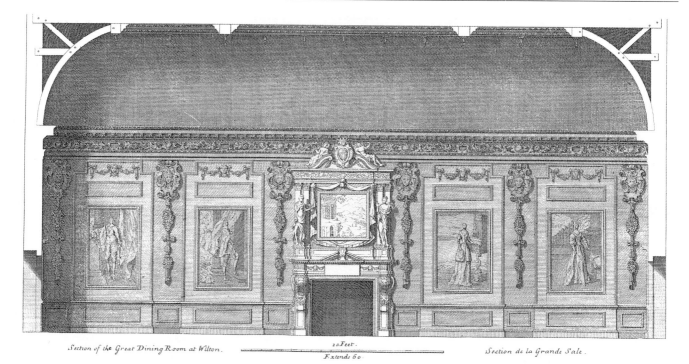

Section of the Great Dining Room at Wilton.   10 Feet.
                                                                  Extends 60.   *Section de la Grande Sale.*

44 Double Cube Room: long section, showing north wall. (Colen Campbell, *Vitruvius Britannicus*, ii, 1717)

from the drawings and engravings of Barbet, Le Pautre and Jean Cotelle, and Evelyn's description of the Wilton chimney-pieces as being 'after the French best manner' was entirely just. The south front state rooms provide us with a clue to what might have been if Webb's Greenwich had been internally fitted up, or his Whitehall built. French inspiration lies behind all his chimney-pieces in these rooms despite, according to Campbell, their being carved in Italy.[49] The opulence of the arrangements employed, the richness of texture, the sudden projections, broken cornices and curving pediments, the swelling, bulbous garlands and swags, is in such great contrast with the reticence of the exterior that the house could be a programmatic illustration of Inigo Jones's well-known dictum contrasting exterior gravity with interior fire.[50]

Of the seven rooms on the main floor of the south front recorded by Campbell, the Cabinet Room in the south-east corner, the King's Room (now the Colonnade Room) and the Double and Single Cube Rooms [**44, 45**] retain their chimney-pieces by Webb. There are plainer chimney-pieces of the same period in the upper rooms of the south-east tower. Two more, in the Ante Room, adjoining the Double Cube Room and in the Little Ante Room next to the Cabinet Room, are eighteenth-century, incorporating seventeenth-century features.

The Drawings

The documentation for the interior of Wilton presents us with numerous problems, being variously partial, conflicting or non-existent. Thus we find that there are ceiling designs which have inscriptions by both Inigo Jones and John Webb, four of them apparently for the same room. None of these ceilings survives. There are designs for doors which carry inscriptions by both Jones and Webb; a further series of designs by Webb for composite capitals; and, lastly, two fine drawings by Webb for wall panelling which might not be for Wilton at all. There must have been many more drawings, now lost. All the surviving titled drawings relate to south range rooms.

a Scale of 30 Feet

Section of the Salon. *One End of the Great Dining Room.*

The existence of drawings for ceilings and doors inscribed by both Jones and Webb poses problems of authorship and of dating. The drawings of state room doors and their copious annotations are in Webb's hand but they carry superscriptions by Jones.[51] The six drawings present designs for almost all the doors on the main floor of the south front, including the blind ones, from the King's Bedchamber through the passage to the 'Great Room' (the Double Cube) [46, 47], then into the 'Withdrawing Room' (the Single Cube), and lastly both into the Passage Room in the south-west corner of the house, and into 'ye old house' (the west wing). The 'Principall doure for the Great roome' carries the explanatory inscription in pencil by Webb: 'towards ye Stayres'.

The titling of the drawings demonstrates Jones's involvement in the fitting up of the south front state rooms, and Webb's annotations confirm that the rooms were arranged in the manner recorded by Campbell. As it would be implausible to suppose a Jones presence

after 1647, it is likely that the laying out of the plan was the work of the 1630s.

There is some evidence to suggest that Webb re-used these drawings in his post-fire refitting. His initial inscriptions are in pencil, most of them being overlaid in ink, so it is at least possible that the annotations were done in two quite separate phases. Rather stronger evidence for re-use is provided by his note 'for Mr Kennard', perhaps the Thomas Kinward who from 1660 until his death in 1682 was Master Joiner of the King's Works.[52] This inscription appears to be in a later hand than the others and is written with a finer pen.

Thus, it is proposed that Jones's 'advice and approbation' during the period of de Caus's work in the later 1630s involved the employment of his assistant, John Webb, on the designing of doors for a state suite, and that the younger man re-used the drawings ten years later when he was employed again at Wilton after the fire. A consideration of the ceiling designs offers further support for this hypothesis.

45 Single Cube Room: section showing north wall (left). Double Cube Room, section showing east wall (right). (Colen Campbell, *Vitruvius Britannicus*, II, 1717)

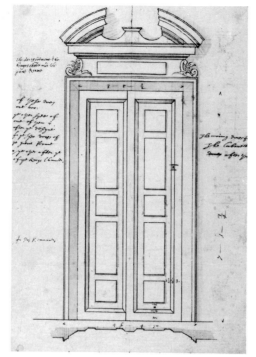

46 John Webb: door between the King's Bedchamber and the Great Room (the Double Cube Room). The inscribed title, upper left, is in Inigo Jones's hand; other inscriptions are by Webb. (WRO, 2057/H1/1a)

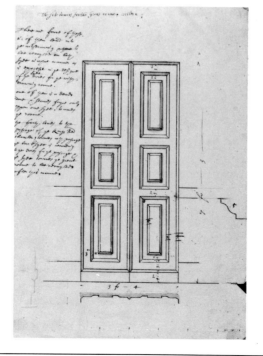

47 John Webb: side doors for the Great Room (the Double Cube Room). Inscriptions as **46** (WRO 2057/H1/1a)

Among the ceiling designs for Wilton in the collection of Worcester College, Oxford, the only dated drawing is by Webb [**48**] and is inscribed by him: 'For ye seeling in ye cabinett Roome Wilton 1649'.[53] A further six designs, for the Great Stairs, the Passage Room into the garden [**49**], the Countess of Pembroke's Bedchamber [**50**], the Countess of Carnarvon's Withdrawing Room and Bedchamber [**51**], and another drawing for the Cabinet Room, have been attributed previously to Jones. In view of Jones's reported reluctance to participate in the overall design of the 1630s house, let alone engage upon the time-consuming task of drawing ceilings, it has been suggested that these drawings could have been made at the behest of his intimate friend, the 3rd Earl, for the old house.[54] Anna Sophia, the 3rd Earl's niece, became Countess of Carnarvon upon her marriage in 1625, and a refitting of her rooms might well have followed. However, the attribution of the drawings to Jones is open to considerable doubt, and it is here suggested that they are by Webb, carried out by him in his capacity as Jones's assistant under the master's direction, and that, together with the doors, they are datable to the later 1630s. At this time Webb was producing his first independent designs, and he was working also as Jones's Clerk Engrosser at old St Paul's Cathedral, which among other administrative duties involved him in 'copying several designs and mouldings and making the tracing according to Mr Surveyor's direction for the workmen to follow'.[55]

The Wilton ceiling drawings do not fit happily in the Jones canon, being marked out fully with a stylus, with ruled pencil lines, and without the strong outline and the freehand verve which one would expect from him, but which one would be surprised to find in the young Webb.[56] The various inscriptions on the drawings for measurements are all in Webb's hand, and the provisional black chalk titling on two of them is discernibly his. When we compare this group with the 1649 Webb ceiling drawing it is apparent that, although the dated one is styled somewhat differently, the drawings have many features in common: the full use of the stylus, the black chalk underdrawing, the pen and wash handling of the schematic drapery and fruit swags and garlands, and the method of noting measurements. Further, the idiosyncratic faces in the border of the Countess of Carnarvon's Bedchamber ceiling lack the liveliness which one would expect from Jones even at this scale. Webb's tentative approach to figure drawing can, however, be paralleled elsewhere in his work.

As designs, the drawings are rather sophisticated for the Webb of the later 1630s. He did not come into his own as a designer of ceilings until he produced his far more densely textured schemes for Greenwich in the 1660s.[57] At Wilton, he was perhaps working under the guidance of Jones, leaning heavily on the drawings of Jean Cotelle, whose contemporary ceiling designs for Parisian *hôtels* appear to have been available to him in the Office of Works.[58] Jones's inscribed titles, as on the drawings of doors, may be read as endorsements of Webb's efforts.

We must now consider the intended locations for the designs. The position of the Cabinet Room is quite clear. According to Webb it measured 18'6" by 21'11", approximately the same dimensions as those recorded by Campbell for the south-east corner room. The projecting chimney-stack on the north wall of this room is acknowledged in both Worcester College drawings, the earlier omitting a small section and the 1649 design carrying a pencilled indication.

There are two further alternative schemes by Webb for the ceiling of the Cabinet Room, both represented by quarter plans and both dated 1649. One, in the collection of the RIBA,[59] for 'ye Cabinett Room' is for an illusionist treatment, and the other, in the Ashmolean Museum, 'for ye vault of ye Ceelings of ye Roomes East and West end', shows a proposed layout for a painted scheme for a ceiling coving.[60]

48 John Webb: design for the ceiling of the Cabinet Room, dated 1649. (Worcester College, Oxford)

49 John Webb: design for the ceiling of the Passage Room, later the Hunting Room. (Worcester College, Oxford)

50 John Webb: design for the ceiling of the Countess of Pembroke's Bedchamber, possibly in the south-west tower. (Worcester College, Oxford)

51 John Webb: design for the ceiling of the Countess of Carnarvon's Withdrawing Room, possibly in the south-east tower. (Worcester College, Oxford)

52 The Cabinet Room: ceiling painted by Andien de Clermont with (*inset*) Luca Giordano's *The Conversion of St Paul*

53 The Chinese Paper Room: situated over the Hunting Room in the south-west tower

54 Double Cube Room: detail of overmantel showing Webb's capitals and the statue of Ceres

55 Double Cube Room: detail of overmantel showing Webb's capitals and the statue of Bacchus

The number of alternative schemes for the Cabinet Room is an indication of its importance, but also an illustration of how many drawings for other rooms must have been lost. The present ceiling in this room has a surround above the Webb cornice painted by Andien de Clermont with an inset central painting by Luca Giordano, *The Conversion of St Paul* [**52**]. This was recorded in 1731 as being 'on the Stair-case by the Great Hall', but was resited in the later 1730s by de Clermont who was paid £130 in 1739 for painting ceilings.[61]

The room at the west end of the south front, the opposite end from the Cabinet Room, was the 'passage room in to ye Garden' which now forms part of the Hunting Room. The seventeenth-century ceiling does not survive. The room is slightly wider than the Cabinet Room, a fact which Campbell chooses to ignore in his quest for symmetry in his plan. The ceiling drawing shows it correctly, measuring 23' across. The existence of a design for this room offers further evidence that the designs were made for the 1630s house rather than for the Tudor building, because whilst the Cabinet Room at the south-east corner of the house was within the line of the original building, the room at the opposite end

of the south range was not, being the creation of de Caus.

The other ceiling designs, excepting that for the Great Geometrical Stairs, do not fit precisely any of the rooms on Campbell's plan, but comparisons of approximate dimensions suggest the rooms in the south-east and south-west towers as probable locations. The Countess of Carnarvon's Withdrawing Room is given the same dimensions on Webb's drawing as the Cabinet Room, and could reasonably have been positioned directly above it with a Bedchamber above that. Both these rooms retain their seventeenth-century chimney-pieces. The Countess of Pembroke's Bedchamber, which according to Webb was slightly larger, measuring 23' across, was the same width as the passage room in the south-west tower, and could therefore have been positioned above it with a Withdrawing Room between the two. No trace of seventeenth-century decoration survives in these upper rooms, one of which now has a nineteenth-century chinoiserie treatment [**53**].

This suggested disposition of rooms, if correct, offers further confirmation of the existence of the towers before the remodelling of their profiles by Webb in the late 1640s.

56 John Webb: design for the cartouche 'over ye principall Dore' (of the Double Cube Room), 1649. (*Book of Capitols*, Devonshire Collection, Chatsworth)

57 John Webb: design for a composite capital for the overmantel of the Great Withdrawing Room (the Single Cube Room). (*Book of Capitols*, Devonshire Collection, Chatsworth)

Webb's drawings for emblematic composite capitals for Wilton include designs for the Countess of Carnarvon's Bedchamber and for the Cabinet Room. For the Double Cube or 'Great Roome' he produced two designs, a Herbert wyvern flanked by cornucopias for the overmantel, and a cartouche 'over ye principall Dore' which is surmounted by wyverns supporting a ducal coronet [54–6]. Both of these are dated 1649 and both were constructed and survive.[62] For the Single Cube or 'Great Withdrawing Roome', Webb's design also incorporated the Herbert wyvern [57]. These capitals also survive.

Access to the State Rooms

In its curtailed form, late seventeenth-century Wilton had a preponderance of subsidiary rooms over great rooms, and the system of circulation must have been found wanting in an age when privacy and convenience were becoming increasingly the desiderata in house planning. Roger North, in the writings on architecture which he made in the 1690s,[63] noted the desirability of the main stairs being separated from the service stairs, and of avoiding the accidental contact between members of the household which was inevitable in a house in which all rooms were through rooms. He was not alone in recognising what we would now consider to be the determinist potential of the house plan for influencing behaviour: Wotton, earlier in the century, had wished to 'avoyd Encounters';[64] Fuller had enjoined the builder to 'Let not thy common rooms be severall, nor thy severall rooms be common';[65] and Pratt wished to be spared the sight of 'servants passing to and fro either to their own inconvenience or to your disturbance'.[66] Wilton, in respect of decorum, would have disappointed all these writers, because its wings were only one room deep and, in the absence of corridors, all its rooms were through rooms. In the mid eighteenth century, proposals were made for courtyard cloister walks, but these had to wait for their implementation until the arrival of Wyatt.[67]

After passing through the great entrance in the east range, the seventeenth-century visitor would have had a choice of routes [58]. Direct access to the south-side state rooms was gained by crossing the court to the ground-floor Stone Hall, next to which the Great Geometrical Staircase rose to the first floor to give access to the Double Cube Room. It would have functioned as a service stair as well as a main stair when the room was fulfilling its function as a grand, formal dining-room, although visitors on those occasions perhaps would have been more likely to take the grand processional route by way of the north and west wings.

Entry into the north range, via the Holbein Porch, would have been into the screens passage which gave on to the Great Hall, unusually, for a house such as this, positioned to one side of the quadrangle rather than directly opposite the entrance gate. At the end of the Hall, a great staircase, hung with paintings, rose to the first floor, where the 'Picture Gallery', in an inventory of 1683, was said to contain fifty-eight pictures.[68] We might expect this to have been a Long Gallery, 'de rigueur in a house of any pretensions',[69] which in such a situation would have fulfilled the triple functions of display, exercise and communication, acting as a corridor through the west wing to the state rooms, and incidentally providing access to the chapel gallery to the west. A gallery decorated with tapestries and paintings was seen by Hammond in 1635, but we cannot be certain that this arrangement continued in the later seventeenth century, for Campbell's plan of 1717 shows the main floor of the west wing subdivided with rooms of 22' by 35' at the southern end, and 22' by 40' at the northern, separated by a small room of 22' by 18'. De Caus might have been responsible for the subdivision at the time he built the projecting chapel. If he was, then the northernmost of these rooms, the largest, might have been the one to be designated the 'Picture Gallery'. Later, in the eighteenth century, these rooms were used for the display of the 8th Earl's large collection of marble statuary,[70] prior to being knocked into one by Chambers during the formation of the library, which occupied the whole of the main floor of the wing.

For his chapel design [59], de Caus clearly was indebted to Inigo Jones's Queen's Chapel at St James's Palace. His elevation drawing[71] shows him considering placing the east end of the building on a line with the end of the reduced south front, but as built, according to

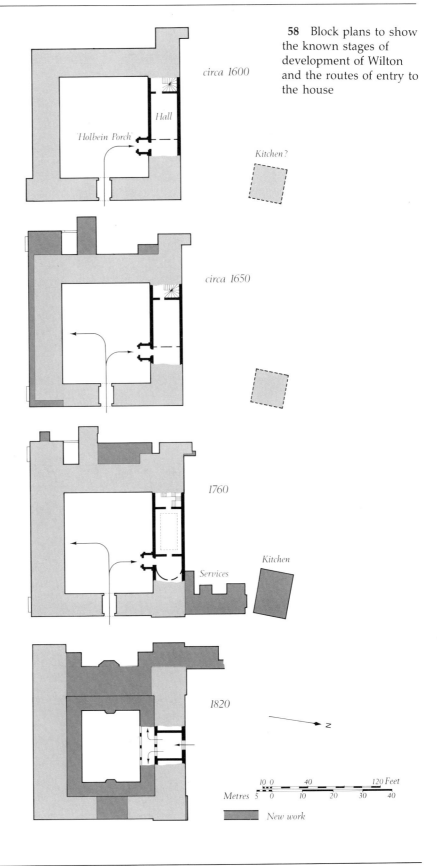

58 Block plans to show the known stages of development of Wilton and the routes of entry to the house

59 Isaac de Caus: side elevation of proposed chapel. This drawing shows the chapel projecting from the west range of the house, on the line of the end of the reduced south front, a single bay of which is shown. (Worcester College, Oxford)

60 Plan of the first-floor state rooms in the south range, redrawn from the plan in *Vitruvius Britannicus*, II, 1717

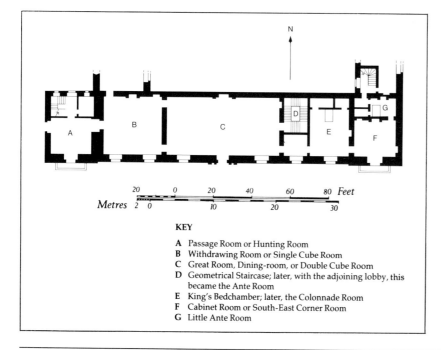

Campbell's plan, it was embedded in the west range with a projection of only 14'.

The chapel gallery was reached at first-floor level by the 22' by 35' room. An untitled ceiling design, which has been associated with Wilton, could be for this room. It is of the correct dimensions and, like the chapel, reliant upon the example of Inigo Jones, in this case the ceiling of the Whitehall Banqueting House, differing only in its central section, where an elongated octagon takes the place of the familiar oval.[72] This design would not have fitted any of the other rooms at Wilton. If it were for this room, it would demonstrate that the layout recorded by Campbell dated at least from the de Caus period, and that despite expectations and the demands of convenience, there was no long gallery in the house after 1635, a situation which was regretted in the later eighteenth century if not earlier. In 1786 it was noted that a gallery really was needed to display the collection of sculpture, but Lord Pembroke had 'made as judicious a disposition as his house would permit'. William Gilpin similarly noted that 'The Hall . . . the staircases, the saloon, and other apartments, might be adorned with a few busts and statues; but to receive the whole collection, perhaps a long gallery should have been professedly built. In this they might have been arranged in profusion'.[73]

The South Front State Rooms

The Single Cube Room, approximately 30' square, is the first which the visitor in the seventeenth century would have entered in the sequence of state rooms [**60**]. The decoration of this, and all the succeeding rooms on the south front, dates from after the 1647 fire, and appears to have been completed by 1654. The Single Cube, [**61, 62, 64**] and the adjoining Double Cube Room [**63**] which measures approximately 60' by 30' by 30', are recognised as the grandest surviving rooms of the mid seventeenth century in England, although not all that we see is in fact of that date. Both rooms retain

KEY

A Passage Room or Hunting Room
B Withdrawing Room or Single Cube Room
C Great Room, Dining-room, or Double Cube Room
D Geometrical Staircase; later, with the adjoining lobby, this became the Ante Room
E King's Bedchamber; later, the Colonnade Room
F Cabinet Room or South-East Corner Room
G Little Ante Room

61 Single Cube Room: the west and north walls

62 Single Cube Room: Webb's chimney-piece and overmantel, with Sir Peter Lely's portrait of Henriette de Kerouaille, Countess of Pembroke (wife of the 7th Earl)

63 Double Cube Room: Webb's chimney-piece and overmantel, with Van Dyck's painting of Charles, James and Mary, children of King Charles I

64 Single Cube Room: overmantel detail showing Webb's composite capitals

65 Double Cube Room: the door to the Ante Room. This originally gave on to the Geometrical Staircase. For the cartouche, *see* **56**

their Webb overmantels and chimney-pieces after Barbet [**63**][74] and their richly carved swags and pendants set on to pine panelling. The carving in the Double Cube Room is the more fully modelled, although it is without the dramatic undercutting of the later seventeenth century. It is not entirely clear how much of this work is original; some certainly dates from the Wyatt period, although it is based on the original scheme. Campbell's long section of the Double Cube, which he calls the Great Dining-Room, does not show the decoration in the inset panels above the Herbert family portraits, perhaps for reasons of taste, perhaps because they were originally blind. The large central doors in the east wall, framed by a magnificent columned doorcase [**65**], originally gave on to the staircase, removed by Wyatt in the creation of the Ante Room, and the flanking, smaller doors, one into the passage and one dummy, were removed at the same time. The panelling therefore had to be in part renewed, and in May 1811, a Salisbury builder, Mr Fisher, submitted estimates for, among other things, work on the panelling of this room. In 1816 the floors in the south front rooms were taken up and relaid following an outbreak of dry rot, and in 1826 the doors in both Cube Rooms were replaced, a bill for the work being submitted by Richard Westmacott.[75] After another outbreak of dry rot in 1948, and the discovery of the splayed jamb of a hitherto concealed medieval or Tudor window in the north-east corner of the Single Cube Room, a door was inserted at this point to provide access to Wyatt's cloisters.

The painted decoration of both rooms is of the mid seventeenth century. The ceiling cove grotesques in oil on plaster in the Single Cube Room are comparable with those in the Queen's House, Greenwich, and can be attributed to the same artist, Matthew Gooderick, who died *c.* 1654. The paintings in the wainscot below the chair-rail, by Emanuel de Critz, depict scenes from Sir Philip

Sidney's *Arcadia* which is said to have been written at the house. De Critz appears to have worked with Webb before, at the Earl of Pembroke's town house in Whitehall where, in 1642, he was paid £3 2s 0d 'upon a bill signed by Mr Webb for painting at the Cockpitt'.[76] The central ceiling panel by Giuseppe Cesari [66], the Cavaliere d'Arpino, is said to have been brought from Florence for the 4th Earl by Sir Charles Cotterell.[77] Its subject matter would have been ironically appropriate after the fire: *Daedalus and Icarus*.

De Critz was also responsible for the three canvases of scenes from the legend of Perseus in the ceiling of the Double Cube Room: *Perseus rescuing his mother from Polydectes* [67], flanked by *Perseus and Andromeda* and *Perseus and Pegasus*.[78] The 10' deep coving was painted in oil on plaster by Edward Pierce: large cartouches with the Pembroke arms are flanked by vases of fruit and putti holding swags.[79]

The Double Cube Room has been rightly praised as 'without question the noblest room of the period (in England) and perhaps the most distinguished in any English country house', although it is equally true that the decorative work 'is unworthy of the architecture and carving with which it was conceived and, compared with the work of contemporary painters in Italy, France and Holland, lamentably provincial'.[80] Chambers again had some pertinent criticisms to make when he turned his attention to this room. He found the coving too deep and the whole ceiling indifferently painted. Except in very clear weather the room was too dark, having only three windows, and the arch of the central window 'cuts off the entablature & rises into the cove very disagreeably' [68].[81] (The 11th Earl made a note in 1809–10 to correct this solecism by blocking the upper part of the window and continuing the entablature, but nothing was done.[82]) Chambers went on to criticise the chimney-piece as 'an exceeding clumsy performance', and the great door, although

66 Single Cube Room: the ceiling. The painting of the coving is attributed to Matthew Gooderick; the inset, *Daedalus and Icarus*, is by Guiseppe Cesari

67 Double Cube Room: the central panel of the ceiling, *Perseus rescuing his mother from Polydectes*, is by Emanuel de Critz

well designed, was marred for him by the broken pediment 'loaded with party coloured arms & gilt muslins intended for representations of the human figure'.

The climax in the painting of the Double Cube Room is provided by the magisterial and far from provincial Van Dyck group portrait, *The Herbert Family*, which hangs on the west wall [**69**]: 'containing thirteen figures as big as the life . . . the painter has reached so near to nature, that one almost imagines it is real life.'[83] Measuring 11' by 17', it was painted *c.* 1634 to *c.* 1636, and hung at the Old Durham House before being moved to Wilton, presumably after July 1654 (for if Evelyn had seen it in place at that time he would surely have mentioned it).[84] If it had always been the

Pembroke intention to display the picture at Wilton, and its perfect fit suggests that it was, then the need for a room of suitable dimensions was probably apparent right from the beginning of the first stage of building by de Caus.

The Double Cube as published by Campbell is symmetrical: the fireplace in the centre of the north wall faces a central Venetian window (without the customary side lights), from which entry to the garden could be made down a double flight of steps. Campbell was correcting what he found. The window in fact opened on to a balcony, the steps being not here but at the west end. Campbell's suggestion for central steps was taken up in 1757 by the 10th Earl, when William Privett was asked to make an estimate for

68 Double Cube Room: the south wall, with the arch of the central window cutting off the entablature and rising into the ceiling cove

adding them, but no work was done.[85]

Both the central window and the chimney-piece are slightly to the east of the centre of the room, the window by a distance of 3' and the fireplace by a distance of 1'. The west and east windows are placed 7' and 2'6'' from their respective corners. The size of the room is such that this asymmetry does not disturb. These internal peculiarities can only be explained by the replanning which was made necessary by the curtailment of the de Caus grand scheme.

Aside from Webb's drawings for capitals and cartouche, there are no drawings for the Cube Rooms as decorated by him, but his two highly finished drawings in the Victoria & Albert Museum have been published as being perhaps

for these rooms.[86] In showing treatments for walls 30' wide and one and a half storeys high, one with a central door flanked by panels and the other with side doors and central aedicule, they could conceivably have been intended for the restoration of the west and east walls of the Single Cube Room after the fire, before the decision was taken to construct a coved ceiling. This remains conjectural, for whilst the standard of decoration proposed would fit the requirements of Wilton, we would expect to see the incorporation of the Herbert wyverns rather than the emblematic eagles. These are more suggestive, among Webb's other known commissions, of the Earl of Peterborough's Drayton in Northamptonshire.[87]

69 Double Cube Room: the west and north walls. Van Dyck's portrait of the Herbert family, commissioned by the 4th Earl, is on the west wall

In Webb's scheme, beyond the Double Cube Room was his Great Geometrical or Hanging Staircase, rising from the ground to the first floor, referred to by Evelyn as 'artificial winding stayres of stone'. Such stairs were normally on a circular or oval plan, Inigo Jones's Tulip Staircase at the Queen's House being an example, but the square plan was not unknown, and Neve offers a description of the form: 'These wind round a Square Newel, either solid, or open . . . and the fore side of each Stair is a right Line pointing to the Centre of the Newel'.[88] A survey made between *c*. 1755 and *c*. 1760 (see p 62), shows that it was lit by two windows in the north wall. Webb's drawing shows that its ceiling was coved and evidence of such coving survives in the present roof.

70 Ante Room: the site of the original Geometrical Staircase. The insertion of the fireplace and the painting of the ceiling both date from the Wyatt period. The door at the north end of the room gives on to Wyatt's cloister

The walls of the staircase were painted 'in Arabesco' by de Clermont,[89] but this decoration disappeared with the stair when Wyatt created his Ante Room [70] out of the stair compartment and the adjoining passage room and inserted another room at second-floor level above. A fireplace was inserted opposite the door into the Double Cube Room, a door was cut through in the north-east corner of the new room to provide access to the cloisters, and niches were inserted at the room's north-west and south-west corners. The ceiling painting, of light clouds in a pale blue sky, surrounded by trellis work and festoons of roses, was painted in oil on plaster by Thomas Ward in a conscious pastiche of the de Clermont manner. He submitted his bill for this work in 1816.[90]

De Clermont himself was responsible for the painted ceiling decoration of the King's Bedchamber (the Colonnade Room) [71, 75] and the Cabinet Room (the Corner Room) [74].[91] Both rooms retain their Webb chimney-pieces after Barbet [73, 72], and the Cabinet Room retains its cornice, but there is no surviving evidence here for a ceiling by Webb. The King's Bedchamber chimney-piece incorporates the Herbert wyverns in its decorative carving. The room was remodelled *c*. 1735 when the closets at its north end were removed and a colonnade inserted, probably to the design of the Architect Earl. Wyatt contemplated the destruction of this room but eventually settled for decorative embellishments.[92] The panelling now is ill-fitting at the angles of the room and has obviously been tampered with, whether during the 1730s or 1800s is unclear.

71 Colonnade Room: formerly the King's Bedchamber

72 (above left) Cabinet Room: Webb's chimney-piece and overmantel, with Gerrit van Honthorst's portrait of Prince Rupert

73 (below left) Colonnade Room: Webb's chimney-piece and overmantel, with *The Madonna*, by Sassoferrato and Mario de'Fiori. The Herbert wyverns appear in the carving of the chimney-piece

74 (above right) Cabinet Room, at the south-east corner of the house. Giordano's *The Conversion of St Paul* is framed by a surround by Andien de Clermont

75 (below right) Colonnade Room: the ceiling painted by Andien de Clermont

76 Little Ante Room: the last in the sequence of state rooms

The last in the sequence of state rooms to be decorated by Webb, the Little Ante Room next to the Cabinet Room [**76, 77**] retains its very free ceiling plasterwork of *c.* 1650, possibly inspired by Le Pautre,[93] which now frames Sabbatini's *Birth of Venus*. This was removed from 'the Cube painted room' and installed here after 1731, possibly by de Clermont in the later 1730s, and certainly by 1751.[94]

At the west end of the south front, the Passage Room to the garden (with wooden steps leading down) and an adjoining staircase have been remodelled to form the Hunting Room [**78**]. A mid seventeenth-century drawing at Wilton for a wall with inset panels differs in detail from the room as constructed but it might represent a scheme for the treatment of the wall between Passage Room and stair.[95] The present double order of panelling has an entablature decorated with shields supported by the wings of the Herbert wyvern. The panelling itself frames eighteen inset panels of hunting scenes by Edward Pierce, which alternate

77 Little Ante Room: the ceiling plasterwork of *c.* 1650 framing Sabbatini's *Birth of Venus*

with hunting trophies attributed to de Clermont.[96] According to Celia Fiennes, the ceiling also was painted with sporting scenes in the seventeenth century.[97] It is generally presumed that the present Hunting Room was created between 1717, the date of Campbell's plan, and *c*. 1735 when de Clermont was employed; in fact the original arrangement survived until 1802–3, when Wyatt replaced the staircase with a new stair in an adjoining tower. He suggested that the newly extended Hunting Room could be 'made use of as a breakfast room or supper room, or dinner room for a small company'.[98] The panelling was reset, and a new ceiling painted in the same de Clermont pastiche style as the ceiling in the Ante Room. Here, the pale blue sky with light clouds is surmounted by a broad, dark green border of garlands in a brown frieze, interspersed with rosettes and ribbons. The new stair rose from the ground to the second floor, with a stair in the main body of the tower continuing to the upper chamber floor.

Accommodation and Services

Visitors to Wilton understandably laid stress upon the architecture and the collections in their comments, neglecting such mundane matters as the provision of accommodation and services. Aubrey however offers us some clues:

'Tis certain that the Earles of Pembroke were the most popular peers in the West of England; but one might boldly say, in the whole kingdome. The revenue of his family was, till about 1652, 16,000 li per annum; but, with his offices and all, he had thirty thousand pounds per annum, and, as the revenue was great, so the greatness of his retinue and hospitality was answerable. One hundred and twenty family uprising and down lyeing, whereof you may take out six or seven, and all the rest servants and retayners.[99]

Even if we allow for exaggeration, these remarks indicate that the accommodation required at Wilton in the seventeenth century was very considerable. The inventory of 1683 lists a substantial

78 Hunting Room: created by Wyatt in a remodelling of the Passage Room and an adjoining staircase. Wyatt's new staircase, placed in a separate tower, is visible through the north door

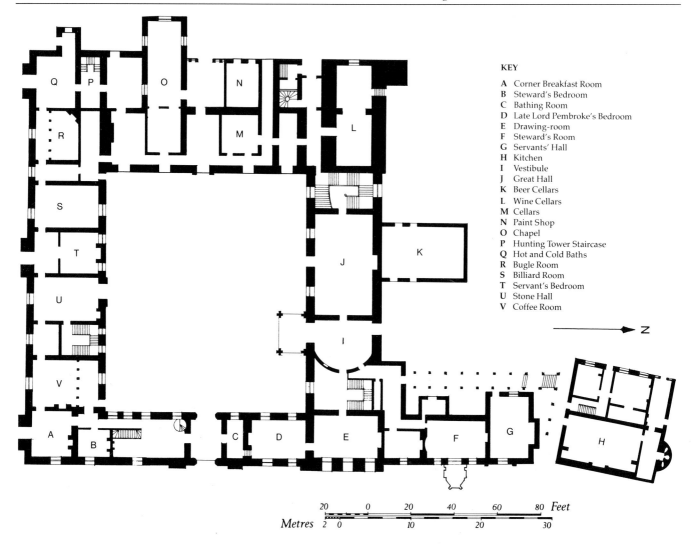

KEY

A Corner Breakfast Room
B Steward's Bedroom
C Bathing Room
D Late Lord Pembroke's Bedroom
E Drawing-room
F Steward's Room
G Servants' Hall
H Kitchen
I Vestibule
J Great Hall
K Beer Cellars
L Wine Cellars
M Cellars
N Paint Shop
O Chapel
P Hunting Tower Staircase
Q Hot and Cold Baths
R Bugle Room
S Billiard Room
T Servant's Bedroom
U Stone Hall
V Coffee Room

79a Wilton House, ground-floor plan: a reconstruction of the mid eighteenth-century layout, based on Rocque's engraved plan (1746) and on plans in the Wilton House archives

number of rooms within and without the main body of the house, but their precise location is seldom clear as the route taken by the compilers is elusive. Further evidence is provided by the plans published by Campbell (1717), the plans published by Rocque in 1746 and the two important mid eighteenth-century plans which carry keys identifying the rooms on the ground and first floors. Neither of these plans is dated but they are datable to *c.* 1755 to *c.* 1760 from internal evidence. (Reconstructions of the mid eighteenth-century plans, together with comparative modern plans are reproduced as **79** and **80**.) The ground plan[100] shows the alterations which can be attributed to the 9th Earl, along with those decorative works which were carried out

in the main state rooms. These include the insertion of colonnades in two of the south side rooms, in the coffee room underneath the Colonnade Room, and in the bugle room underneath the Single Cube Room. Reference is made on the key to the plan to the 'Late Lord Pembroke's Bd. Room', and a date soon after the death of the 9th Earl in 1750 thus appears likely. The plan certainly cannot have been produced much later than 1755, because the 'Passage to the Riding house', so marked, is for the building at some distance to the north of the house, replaced by the new building begun in that year.[101]

The first-floor plan[102] assigns a bedroom in the east range to Sir Andrew Fountaine, who died in 1753, but it is

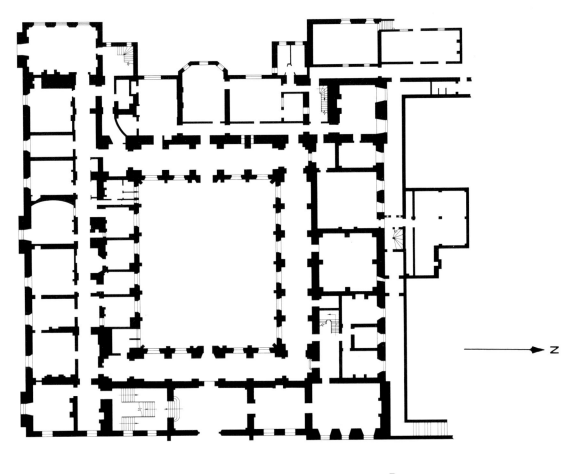

20   0   20   40   60   80 *Feet*

Metres 2 0   10   20   30

Z

nonetheless datable to *c*. 1755 to *c*. 1760 because it shows the 'New Library' in the west wing designed by Sir William Chambers. It would not be unreasonable to suppose that Sir Andrew's room continued to be known by his name some years after his death as he had been a very important member of the household. He had been responsible for obtaining Italian paintings for the 8th Earl, 'bespoke when Sir And. Fountaine was in Italy', to replace some of the German and Flemish collection at Wilton, and he continued to act as librarian and custodian of works of art to the 9th Earl.[103] His bust by Roubiliac survives in the house, placed in Wyatt's gothic entrance hall [81].[104]

Both of these mid eighteenth-century plans represent the house as it appeared in 1801 when Wyatt started work. The ground plan carries the endorsement 'Ground plan of Wilton House as it remained in March 1801', and the first-floor plan corresponds in all important particulars with a survey of *c*. 1801 which was made for Wyatt.[105] The available evidence is such that we can be more confident about the precise placing of the accommodation towards the end of the eighteenth century than we can about the previous century, but nevertheless certain broad conclusions can be drawn, particularly if we bear in mind the common monastic arrangement of buildings around a courtyard which the later Wilton might well have perpetuated in part.

79b Modern ground-floor plan, based on RCHME investigation

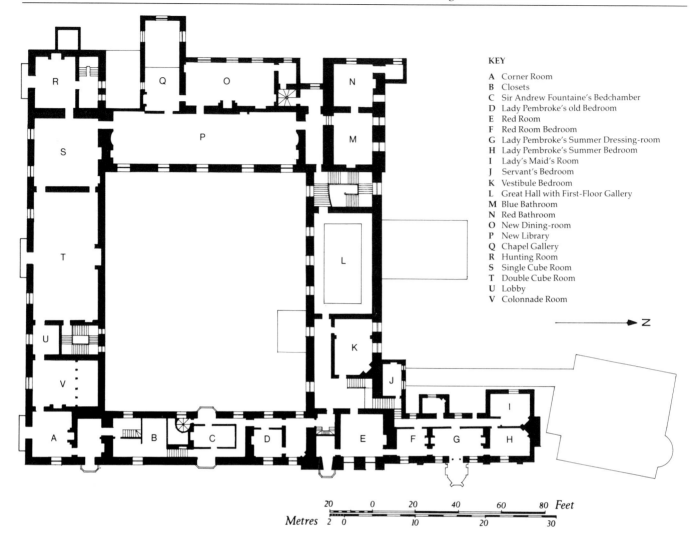

KEY

A Corner Room
B Closets
C Sir Andrew Fountaine's Bedchamber
D Lady Pembroke's old Bedroom
E Red Room
F Red Room Bedroom
G Lady Pembroke's Summer Dressing-room
H Lady Pembroke's Summer Bedroom
I Lady's Maid's Room
J Servant's Bedroom
K Vestibule Bedroom
L Great Hall with First-Floor Gallery
M Blue Bathroom
N Red Bathroom
O New Dining-room
P New Library
Q Chapel Gallery
R Hunting Room
S Single Cube Room
T Double Cube Room
U Lobby
V Colonnade Room

| | 20 | 0 | 20 | 40 | 60 | 80 | *Feet* |
| *Metres* | 2 | 0 | | 10 | | 20 | 30 |

80a Wilton House, first-floor plan: a reconstruction of the mid eighteenth-century layout, based on Rocque's engraved plan (1746) and on plans in the Wilton House archives

It will be recalled that, when de Caus was about to begin his building work in 1636, the housekeeper was required to empty the lodgings on the south side of the house, and it appears from Campbell's plan that the rebuilding to some extent followed this arrangement as he shows beds in several of the rooms on the ground floor of this wing. By the mid eighteenth century only one of these rooms, in the centre of the range, remained as a bedroom. The west end room below the Hunting Room had become a hot and cold bathroom, the two rooms at the east end had become breakfast and coffee rooms, and a billiard room had been fitted up next to the servant's bedroom under the Double Cube Room. Only the Stone Hall appears to have retained its original function.[106]

As we have noted, some family accommodation appears to have been provided in the upper rooms of the south-east and south-west towers. Further family rooms were probably located in the east wing, the customary site of monastic lodgings. It was here in the eighteenth century that Lord Pembroke had his bedroom and adjacent drawing-room on the ground floor (the present little and large smoking rooms), and Lady Pembroke had her equivalent apartments on the floor above. Here also, on the first floor, Sir Andrew Fountaine was housed.

The north range, built partly on the site of the abbey church, contained the Great Hall and, in the eighteenth century, the apsed vestibule where marble

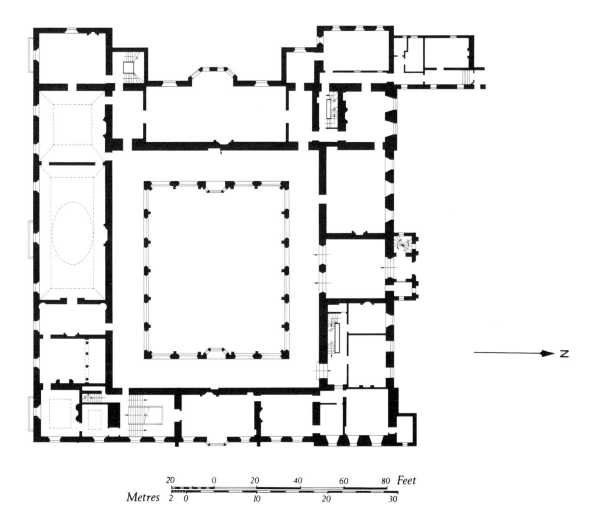

20   0   20   40   60   80 *Feet*

Metres 2 0   10   20   30

80b Modern first-floor plan, based on RCHME investigation

statuary was displayed. Beyond, after the grand staircase at the west end of the range, were the wine cellars, housed within the massively thick walls which survived from the monastic buildings. The remainder of the lower floor of the west range, as far south as the chapel, also comprised cellar storage space, which again followed the usual monastic scheme. Above, on the first floor, the west wing was used for display rather than for accommodation. By the mid eighteenth century, the collection was such that more and more rooms had to be pressed into service to house it. Hanway, visiting in 1755, observed that:

> The lower apartments are so crouded, that they appear like so many shops or magazines of marble merchandize. But amidst this profusion of grandeur, the arrangement seems to be as elegant as such a number will admit . . . [107]

The main service rooms, in the seventeenth and eighteenth centuries, were on the ground floor of the continuation of the east wing, beyond the main block of the house, which formed the side of a base court to the north. Here *c.* 1755 were the servants' hall and the steward's room, close to Lord Pembroke's rooms, an arrangement which Roger North would have approved as it enabled the master 'who I doe not suppose to be above economy', occasionally to oversee the servants and 'transact with them, and other mean persons, without concerning his guest, or anoying the principall, and enterteining part of his house'.[108]

81 Gothic entrance hall, ground floor of east range, looking towards Wyatt's staircase. Roubiliac's bust of Sir Andrew Fountaine is in the far right-hand corner of the room. (*Country Life*)

Next to the servants' hall, linked to the house by a pentice or covered way, was a large detached kitchen and its offices. This medieval arrangement continued until the time of Wyatt's alterations. According to Rocque's eighteenth-century plan of the house, the drawing-room at the north-east corner was earlier used as a dining-room, conveniently situated near the kitchen and presumably used daily by the family, who would be inclined to use the more distant great dining-room, the Double Cube Room, only on formal occasions. Reference is made in the 1683 inventory to a further 'old kitchen' which appears, from its position in the list, to have been to the north-west of the great staircase in the north range, but there is no trace of it in the mid eighteenth-century plans and its precise position cannot be ascertained. Later, after Chambers' alterations, there was a new dining-room in the west range, at some distance from the detached kitchen. This could conceivably have been served by the 'old' kitchen, if it survived until that time.

Despite being a house of considerable size, Wilton does not seem to have had extensive provision for accommodation, being hampered in part by having ranges of only single room depth. There was a shortage of both important family apartments and of servants' rooms. We must presume, given the numbers recorded by Aubrey, that there was further accommodation for servants in garrets, in the group of older ancillary buildings to the north-west of the house which are shown in the drawing of 1669 and also, probably, in the Tudor gatehouse.[109]

The Eighteenth-Century House

On 11 March 1705 John Evelyn entered into his diary:

> Exceeding dry season: Greate losse by fire by the burning of the out-houses & famous stable, at Burley . . . by carelessnesse of a servant; as most of these accidents happen by, & in a little before at Wilton my L. Pembrocks

Campbell offers more details:

> The Hall Side being burnt . . . was rebuilt by the present Thomas Earl of Pembroke, then Lord High Admiral of England, in a very noble and sumptuous Manner.[110]

The rebuilt north range is recorded for us in Campbell's plan. From the Holbein Porch, entry was made into the Great Hall via the large, apsed vestibule lined with niches, which replaced the original screens passage. The hall was two storeys high, with a first-floor gallery which a later visitor likened to the one at Houghton.[111] This served the dual purpose of display and a corridor link between the east and west ends of the wing. It is likely that the opportunity was taken at this time to rebuild the north side towers, giving them the same profile as those on the south. Both towers have a cavetto string course, probably of early eighteenth-century date, and the north-east tower still has its eighteenth-century roof timbers. The north-west tower retained its thick medieval walls in the two lower storeys. All four towers are shown alike on Stukeley's drawing of 1723.[112]

The room at the foot of the north-east tower, the present large smoking room [82], was given a marble chimney-piece at this time. In an account published in 1766, it was said to be by Inigo Jones, but along with the rest of the decoration in this room, and in the adjoining little smoking room [83], it is more securely datable to the early eighteenth century.[113]

Campbell does not name the architect of the new work, but the classical splendour of the north side internal arrangement, which provided a very appropriate setting for the large collection of classical sculpture amassed by Thomas, the 8th Earl, suggests the hand of a man in sympathy with the ideals of Jones and Webb. The design might be attributed to John James, who not only is known to have admired the work of Jones for showing that 'the Beautys of Architecture may consist with the greatest plainness of the structure', but he also included the name of the Earl of Pembroke in a list of names of those 'Persons of Quality' who could vouch for his character, many of whom he had 'served in the business of their Buildings'.[114] The reference does not provide conclusive evidence, for James

82 Large smoking room: ground floor of the east range, in the north-east tower

83 Little smoking room: between the gothic hall and the large smoking room

was working on carpentry at Wilton church between *c*. 1700 and 1710, an employment for which he might well have been indebted to the Earl of Pembroke, thus justifying his statement. However, it is equally arguable that being a man on the spot, the Earl could have turned to him for assistance after the fire in the house.[115]

After the rebuilding of the north range, various alterations were carried out elsewhere in the house during the course of the eighteenth century. The 9th Earl employed Andien de Clermont on decorative works in the south side state rooms, and he employed Pieter Jan van Reysschoot ('van Risquet') to paint the north side staircase.[116] He also made improvements to the ground-floor rooms of the south range, and improved the access to the cellars in the west range by cutting a corridor through to provide a route along the wing. Rather more significant alterations were carried out for the 10th Earl by Sir William Chambers.

Chambers was responsible for a remodelling of the west range, and in view of his strong criticism of the seventeenth-century work at Wilton, it is unfortunate for our purposes of comparison that his efforts did not survive the Wyatt period, and that the later eighteenth-century visitors did not discuss them. Hanway had been told during his visit in 1755, which he published two years later, that 'the present young Lord intends to build a library, or to convert one of his apartments to that use'.[117] Chambers was paid in 1762 for 'Various Sketches and designs for fitting up a library at Wilton'[118] and the year before John Adair had been paid £92 18s 1d for various doorcases, architraves and mouldings which presumably were related to the Chambers scheme.[119]

The first-floor survey plan shows the house as Chambers left it. He created the library by knocking the three rooms on the main floor of the west range into one long room. He was probably responsible also for the design of the new dining-room, which was built next to the new

library in the angle between the projecting chapel and the north-west tower.

The external appearance of the west and the north ranges in the eighteenth century is not known, but Rocque's engraving shows on the east front gothick features which might be considered to have been the work of the 9th Earl, possibly in collaboration with Roger Morris, with whom he was building the Palladian Bridge in 1736. In addition to his Palladian leanings, Morris had already demonstrated an inclination towards medievalising at Clearwell Castle, a castellated gothick house of *c*. 1728.

A more serious and extensive attempt to recall Wilton's monastic beginnings was commenced in 1801.

The Nineteenth-Century House

In 1798, the entrance to Wilton from the east [84, 85, 87] was described by Gilpin as 'awkward and incumbered'.[120] A large programme of alterations was shortly entrusted by the 11th Earl to James Wyatt who, beginning in 1801, made changes in all four wings of the house. The Earl's aims in these works were threefold: better internal communication and 'a safe retreat from House Gazers',[121] through the provision of corridors around the internal courtyard; a west-facing living-room-cum-library; and direct entry into the north hall rather than via the east gate tower. The Earl of Carnarvon, in a letter to Pembroke, approved of Wyatt's plan. He noted the violence done to the 'monastick charm' of the court 'but out of this act of violence may arise a most beautiful Gothick Cloyster which will obviate all difficulties in communication, and give Beauty, Magnificence & comfort to the House'. In a further letter he expressed the fear 'which is that you who do not feel the difference between a Marquis & an Earl will not feel the wide distinction between a Passage & a Cloyster, & be satisfied with too Little Gothick ornament in that part'. He hoped that 'Wyatt will imitate the simplicity of old Inigo on the outside and bestow the cash

on the Cloysters, Library and Hall'.[122] Perhaps all would have been well if he had, but Wyatt's lack of planning in advance and the absence of proper supervision of the work led to innumerable problems. These culminated in his dismissal in 1810 when Lord Pembroke engaged Mr Fisher of Salisbury to complete the works.

The appearance of the house at this time is described by Louis Simond who visited in July:

A whole wing was dismantled and thrown open ten years ago to make a gallery of antiques. The floors exposed to the injuries of the weather are half-rotten, and the poor antiques, thrown about higgledy-piggledy, sans nose, sans fingers, sans every other prominent member, form a marble field of battle, half melancholy, half ridiculous, the sight of which would distress me beyond measure, were I their master and could not afford to finish the work so unfortunately begun.[123]

Surprisingly, the Wyatt connection with Wilton did not stop in 1810. James's nephew, Jeffry Wyatville, continued to make drawings for the new works, producing designs for the ground-floor breakfast room on the south front in 1814.[124] In 1826 he was consulted about works at Lord Pembroke's Bulbridge House, and before 1851, Thomas Henry Wyatt made further minor alterations at Wilton.[125]

Between 1801 and 1811, £50,000 was spent on James Wyatt's works and a further £20,000 was needed to complete the job.[126] Already, in 1802, Pembroke's steward, John Seagrim, was finding it necessary to warn his employer: 'I never yet knew or heard of a business of this kind but what greatly exceeded the first supposed cost'.[127]

When Lord Pembroke taxed the architect with his non-attendance and the consequent errors in the work, Wyatt protested in a letter of justification,

84 The entrance front from the east, in the eighteenth century. (Bodleian Library, Malchair v, No 8)

85 The east range, formerly the entrance range

86 (below left) Wyatt's cloisters: the north-west corner, seen from the central courtyard, with the well-head in the foreground.

87 (below right) One of the pair of niches which flank the east range entrance

written in 1809, that 'Your Lordship's mind has been poison'd' and that he had given eight or nine years to the improvements.[128] But, as John Seagrim explained in 1816, 'For want of Mr Wyatt's more frequent attendance at Wilton, the Clerks of the Works were often at a loss how to proceed and I understood there were perpetual alterations made in the building . . . from want of Mr Wyatt's instructions . . .'.[129] Wyatt's record of attendance was certainly not good: ten days in 1806, fourteen in 1807 and only three in 1808. And there were frequent grounds for complaint about the quality of the construction: the cloister walks were found to have dry rot; they leaked in eleven different places and rain water cracked the rendering; the library flues caused them to catch fire twice and, most extraordinarily, the new walls of the library had to be taken down in 1816 and carried further out. In the east range, the new staircase had to be taken down and rebuilt shortly after its erection, and in the south range the new basement floor had to be laid twice because of dry rot.[130] The cloisters were still unfinished in 1815, when Richard Westmacott was employed to oversee their completion

and the arrangement within of the paintings and classical busts: 'Your Lordship's resolution to treat the 3 unfinished sides of the Cloister with the simplicity of the North side may certainly be affected without any additional expense or much trouble'.[131]

Notwithstanding the difficulties caused by faulty construction, Wyatt's gothic cloisters [86, 88] were his most effective contribution to Wilton, providing independent internal access to all rooms on the ground and principal floors [90].

The new cloister windows [89] made use of old heraldic glass from the Tudor building, originally installed by the 2nd Earl. These include the arms of Henry VIII and his Queens, and those of the Herbert and Sidney families. Some extra armorial pieces were bought in 1805 from a Mrs Portman and a Mrs Hayter of Salisbury Close. The re-glazing was carried out in 1806–7 by Maria Egginton of Birmingham, an appointment made upon the recommendation of Wyatt.[132]

The insertion of the cloister forced the removal of the Holbein Porch, which was later re-erected in the garden to the west.

Demolition of the original service range to the north-east of the house was begun

88 Interior of Wyatt's first-floor south side cloister, looking east

89 (below right) The north-east corner of Wyatt's first-floor cloister.

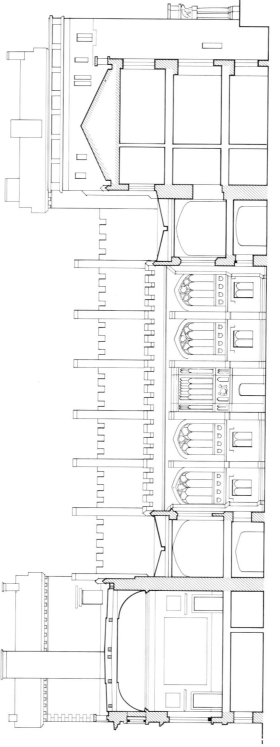

90a Section through the house from south to north, showing the Double Cube Room to the south and *Wyatt's* raised forecourt to the north

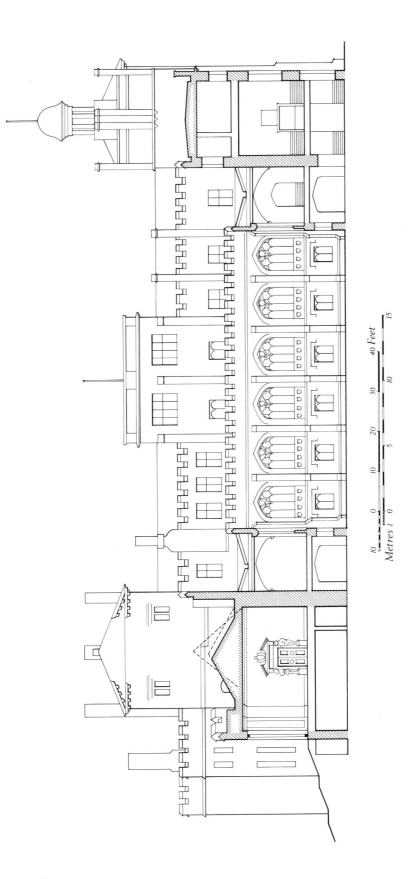

90b Section through the house from west to east. The former library is on the west side, with the projecting chapel beyond. The lines of former roof pitches are shown dotted, above the roof of the library

Metres 1 0   10   0   10   20   30   40 *Feet*

0   5   10   15

91 (right) The Webb chimney-piece, possibly re-sited by Wyatt, situated in the former dining-room, next to the north entrance hall

92 (below left) The west range seen from the Italian garden. Wyatt's chapel is to the left, and his stair tower next to the Hunting Room abuts the south-west tower

93 (far right) One of the baroque doorcases in the former library in the west range

94 (below right) The roof of Wyatt's west range, looking towards the north-west tower

by Wyatt in 1809, prior to the construction of the new north entrance forecourt.[133] He built a new service range on the opposite side of the court, separated from the house by a few open arches to disperse kitchen smells. He situated the dining-room [**91**] at first-floor level, to the west of the new entrance hall, placing it above the servants' hall whose constant fire would, it was felt, contribute greatly to the warmth of the dining-room.[134] The

kitchen subsequently has been brought into the main body of the house, and is now situated on the ground floor of Wyatt's west wing.

The west wing was rebuilt by Wyatt to provide a large Tudor gothic library, with offices below. The library fittings were removed *c*. 1925 to *c*. 1930 and Wyatt's mullioned windows were replaced with sashes. The room is now a drawing-room. Its two baroque doorcases [**93**],

95 (above left) Wyatt's staircase in the east range

96 (above right) The north range, after Warre's alterations

97 (left) Wyatt's north entrance range and forecourt, photographed in the late nineteenth century, before the alterations by Edmund Warre

each with term figures carrying a broken pediment, were brought out of store in the stables at that time. They might have come originally from the rebuilt Great Hall of *c.* 1705, and been removed as being too 'Grecian', a quality which Wyatt was anxious to avoid.[135] The rebuilt west range [92] is lower than the range which it replaced, and Wyatt's work has revealed the line of the former steeply pitched roof in the south face of

the north-west tower [94]. Next to the tower, Wyatt built his gothic chapel, which brought the north range of the house into alignment with the longer south range, and enabled him to frame the composition of his west front. In creating his new entrance and approach from the north [97], Wyatt raised the level of the forecourt by some ten feet, effectively concealing all traces of monastic remains which might have been

98   The Almonry, from the east

99   The Almonry: the south wall, with the Pembroke lion and panther supporters over the doorway

expected to survive there. He added a gothic porte-cochère, which was dismantled *c.* 1914 under the direction of Edmund Warre who also rebuilt the north façade, removing Wyatt's gothic windows and replacing his battlements with a balustrade [**96**].[136] He retained Wyatt's roof: a truss in the eastern side of the north range carries the date 1807.

On the east front, Wyatt remodelled the existing entrance tower and cupola, and raised the linking blocks to the corner towers by one storey. He added the ground-floor entrance known as the Gothic Hall, and removed the eighteenth-century gothic two-storey projecting bay and first-floor oriels. Inside the east range, Wyatt provided the new plain stair [**95**] to the south of his Gothic Hall which replaced Webb's south side Great Geometrical Staircase.

Wyatt's additions and alterations certainly made necessary improvements to the efficiency of Wilton, but it is a matter for considerable regret that he went as far as he did in the romantic pursuit of monastic origins. The losses of the older work in the north and west ranges especially, appear to have been considerable, and pending an unexpected archival discovery, irretrievable.

Related Structures

The Almonry

This fourteenth-century stone structure [**98,99**] is the only surviving building at Wilton of pre-Reformation date.[137] It is to the west of the house, aligned north-south, and has been curtailed at its southern end, the present south wall being of brick inside and probably dating from the Wyatt period. A reset stone panel in this wall has the initials 'WP' (William–Pembroke?) on a shield between the Pembroke lion and panther supporters, positioned over a Wyatt doorway. The largely original roof is of slightly more than four bays in length. The principal trusses have two collars, the lower one with arch braces rising from wall posts and corbels. There are two tiers of purlins, the lower having curved windbraces below.

This building, despite the similarity of its name, cannot be confidently equated with the 'Armoury', which was described by Lieutenant Hammond in 1635 as '60 yards in Length, the number of Armes therein will confidently furnish, and fit out 1000. Foote and Horse'.[138] The Armoury was noted also by Aubrey as 'a very long roome, which I guesse to have

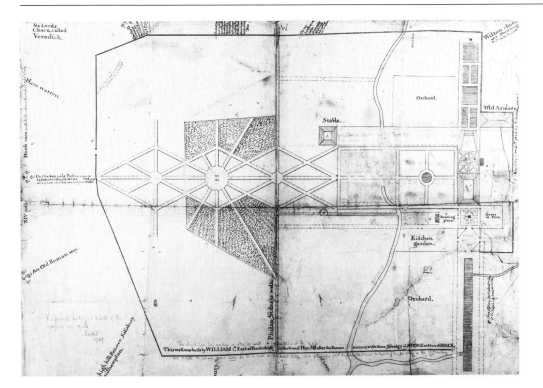

100 Estate plan of *c.* 1700 (WHA)

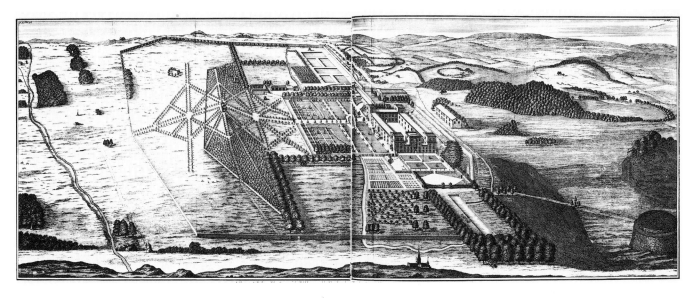

been a dorture heretofore'.[139] The 'Old Armory' is depicted on an estate plan of *c.* 1700 [**100**] to the west of the house, [140] (*see also* Colen Campbell's perspective view [**101**]), but if the Almonry and the Armoury are one and the same, then the building must have been reduced to a third of its original length.

The Holbein Porch
This mid sixteenth-century porch [**102,103**] depicted by Buckler in the central courtyard of the house shortly before its removal, is now situated in the grounds to the west of the house.[141] The *Gentleman's Magazine* reported in 1812 that it 'has lately been destroyed',[142] but its materials had been numbered and

101 Perspective from the east. (Colen Campbell, *Vitruvius Britannicus*, III, 1725)

102   Holbein Porch, in the grounds to the west of the house

103   Holbein Porch, interior

'safely put by'. It was noted in 1819 that some of its carving and busts needed replacement, but its re-erection in the garden did not take place until 1826, at which time a room, since removed, was added at the rear.[143]

East Entrance Lodge and Gates (demolished)
The Tudor gatehouse, depicted on the Survey of the lands of the 1st Earl, survived until the later seventeenth century.[144] It was illustrated in 1669 by

Magalotti,[145] but it had gone by the time of Knyff's painting of *c.* 1700 [**105**].[146] The gatehouse was situated between the formal parterre garden which adjoined the east front and a forecourt further east. Entry into the latter was made through gate-piers [**104**], illustrated by Campbell,[147] which on stylistic grounds can be attributed to John Webb, resembling as they did the gate-piers at Amesbury. They were flanked in the eighteenth century by the stone columns of de Caus's Coronet fountains.

Close to the gates, illustrated in one of Rocque's vignettes [**106**], was the porter's lodge, which has been attributed by John Harris to Roger Morris.[148] Both the gates and the lodge are now gone.

Marble Fountain in the Italian Garden
The presence of the Herbert wyvern and the Sidney porcupine as decorative features upon the fountain suggest that it was made to commemorate the union of the two families which took place in 1577, when Henry, the 2nd Earl, married his third wife, Mary Sidney. Campbell shows the fountain on an hexagonal base in the central court of the house, but by the time of Rocque's survey it had been re-sited in the east forecourt. Now, re-set by Westmacott, it stands in the Italian garden to the west of the house [**107**].[149]

The Stables (Washern Grange)
Aubrey gives a description of the stables in their prime: 'of Roman architecture, built by Mons. de Caus, [they] have a noble avenu to them, a square court in the middle; and on the four sides of this court were the pictures of the best horses as big as the life, painted in severall postures, by a Frenchman'.[150] The de Caus building, of brick and stone, incorporated part of a grange of the former abbey, a fourteenth-century barn [**108**], which was converted into stables and survives, forming the eastern side of the arcaded quadrangle. The western range has been demolished. Campbell ignored the asymmetry of the arrangement in his published plan of the stables, making the

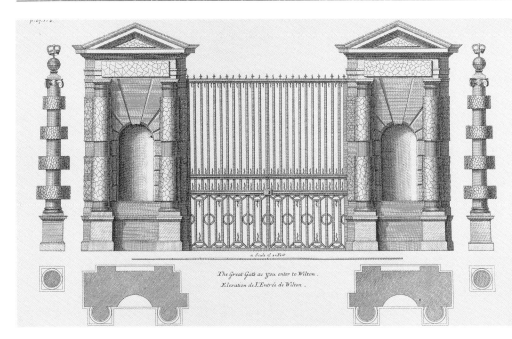

104 John Webb's gates and the Coronet Columns from de Caus's gardens. (Colen Campbell, *Vitruvius Britannicus*, II, 1717)

105 L Knyff's topographical painting of *c*. 1700: bird's eye view from the east with inset panels showing the south side of the house, waterfall and statuary, de Caus's stables and the interior of the Grotto, the Loggia with bowling green, and the Pavilion. (Wilton House)

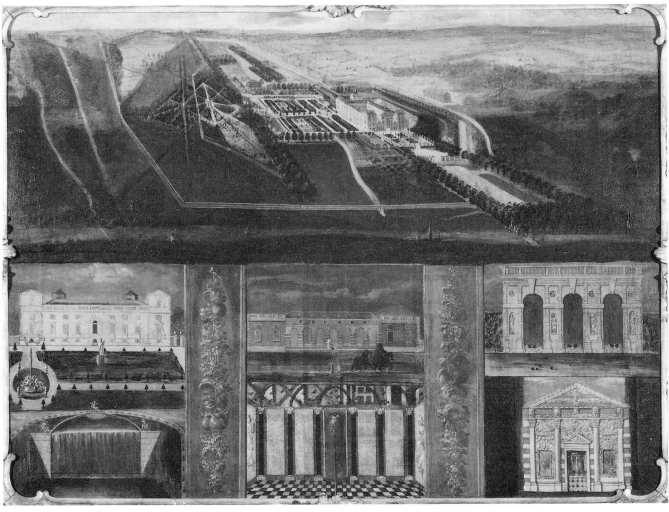

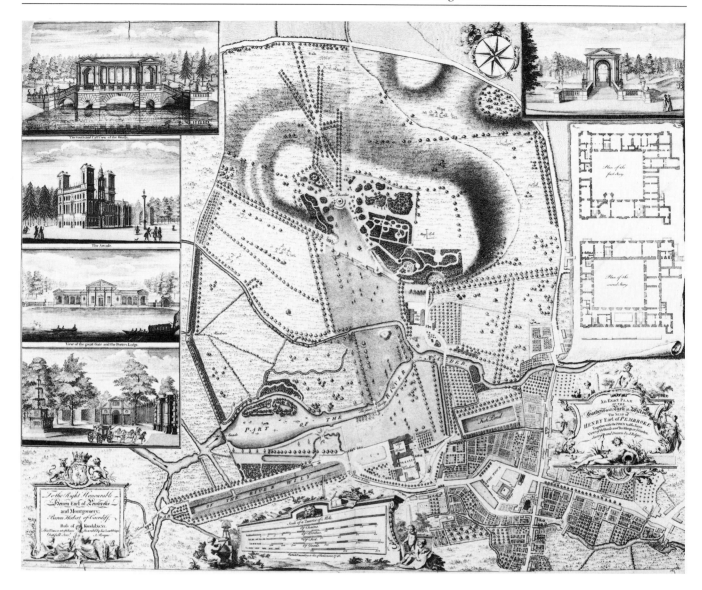

106 J Rocque's plan of the house and garden, 1746, with vignettes of the house, the Palladian Bridge, the arcade at the east end of the lake (which incorporated the pavilion as its centrepiece), the gates and the porter's lodge

east and west ranges identical [**109**].[151]

The north elevation [**110**], visible from the house, has a central, arcaded screen (with later windows) flanked by balustraded pavilions. The building is broadly north Italian in feeling, but the presence of circular and œil-de-bœuf windows recalls the French character of the original de Caus proposals for Wilton House itself.

These stables are interestingly similar in style to those at Ramsbury, an estate which, between 1553 and 1676, was owned by the Earls of Pembroke.[152] Mons de Caus might have been responsible for those as well.

Isaac de Caus's Garden and its related structures
The laying out of the formal gardens at Wilton by Isaac de Caus began in 1632.[153] The original scheme is recorded for us in two elevated prospect drawings looking south and north[154] (the latter also showing the long south front of the proposed new house) and in engravings which the architect published in *Wilton Garden c.* 1654 [**111**]. The engravings do not include the view towards the house, as the grand rebuilding scheme was not carried out, but the prospect to the south, a plan of the garden and details of the fountains, statuary and grotto were all

107 The marble fountain in the Italian garden

108 The barn, which forms the eastern side of the quadrangular stables

Plan and Elevation of the out Offices at Wilton.

Plan et Elevation des Equieries de Wilton.

a Scale of 60 Feet

Extends 125

published with a short commentary. Drawings of panels for the grotto and sections through the elevated terrace in de Caus's hand also survive.[155]

The gardens were first commented upon by Lieutenant Hammond, who appears to have been given a guided tour in 1635 by the architect himself: 'the fat Dutch Keeper . . . a rare Artist'. He was shown 'a fayre House of Freestone . . . at the further end of the . . . Garden, below all Archt, with seats, and pau'd with Freestone; the Roofe flatt, and leaded with Freestone Battlements and Water-Pooles; the Statues of Venus, Luna and 2. more, are cut in white Marble on the Frontispice; Close to this Banquetting House, is that rare Water-worke now making, and contriuing by this outlandish Engineer, for the Singing, and Chirping of Birdes, and other strange rarities, onely by that Element . . .'[156]

The de Caus grotto and gardens survived to be seen by Celia Fiennes in the late seventeenth century,[157] but replanting and rearrangement was already in progress by the time of Knyff's view. The gardens were then landscaped in the later 1730s by the 9th Earl, who dammed the River Nadder (a feature which de Caus had ignored as far as he was able) to create the lake. The Editor of Defoe's *Tour* approved the new arrangement:

109 The Stables: elevation and plan. (Colen Campbell, *Vitruvius Britannicus*, ii, 1717)

110 Isaac de Caus's stables: the north elevation

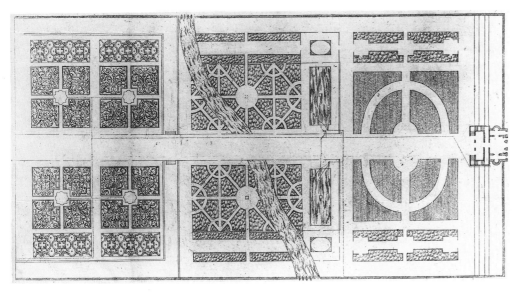

111 Isaac de Caus's garden: the plan, published in *Wilton Garden, c.* 1654

112 The gardens, showing the south front of the house and the Palladian Bridge, in an engraving published in 1759

A View of Wilton in Wiltshire the Seat of the R. Hon. the Earl of PEMBROKE. — Vüe de Wilton dans la Comté de Wilts sa Maison & Jardin magnifique du Comte de PEMBROKE. —

Published according to Act of Parliament, March 1759. — Printed for the Bowles in S. Pauls Church Yard, Ja. Bowles & Son in Cornhill, & I. Tinney in Fleetstreet. —

'The present Earl of Pembroke . . . has made a further Improvement with regard to Prospect . . . throwing down the Walls of the Garden, and making, instead of them, the newly introduced Haw haw Walls, which afford a boundless View all around the Country from every Quarter.'[158] This 'natural' landscape is recorded in Richard Wilson's views which were painted for the 10th Earl in 1758–60 [**112**].[159]

Although Isaac de Caus's garden survives only on paper, many of its individual features are still extant, though relocated.

The Grotto (demolished)
Isaac de Caus's arcaded grotto was set in the middle of a balustraded walk, at the southern end of the long central avenue of the garden. Its internal appearance is preserved for us in de Caus's published plates which show the four bas-reliefs, now sited in the Loggia in the Italian Garden, in their original positions on the side walls of the central space, surmounted by further statuary, all being set in the midst of extravagantly frosted

rustication. Some of de Caus's studies for these decorative panels survive.[160]

The grotto was still functioning well at the time of Celia Fiennes' visit towards the end of the seventeenth century: 'in the middle roome is a round table, a large pipe in the midst, on which they put a crown or gun or a branch, and so it spouts the water through the carvings and poynts all round the roome at the Artists pleasure to wet the Company; there are figures at each corner of the roome that can weep water on the beholders . . . on each side is two little roomes which by the turning their wires the water runnes in the rockes you see and hear it, and also it is so contrived in one room that it makes the melody of Nightingerlls and all sorts of birds which engaged the curiosity of the Strangers to go in to see . . .'[161] This curiosity could only be satisfied at the price of another wetting.

The pressure of water required for all these delights was considerable. Aubrey explains the mechanics: 'By the kitchin garden is a streame which turnes a wheele that moves the engine to raise the water to the top of a cisterne at the corner

113   The Pavilion, now forming the façade of Park School House

of the great garden, to serve the water-workes of the grotto and fountaines in the garden'.[162]

The grotto did not survive into the eighteenth century in its original position. By the time of Knyff's painting it had been re-sited to form the Bowling Green Pavilion south-east of the house and by the time of Lord Oxford's visit in 1738 it had been removed altogether.[163]

The Pavilion (Park School House)

This pavilion [113], to the east of the house, was set up in its present position by Wyatt. It incorporates an elaborately carved façade by de Caus, which was described by Christopher Hussey as a '*tour de force . . . in grotesquerie*'.[164] It is shown in a vignette in Knyff's painting substantially in the form in which we see it today, although there are differences of detail. Knyff shows it as built in brick and stone, with grotesque masks rather than half-length figures over the capitals, and masks rather than rosettes over the side openings. The Francophile decorative vocabulary is consistent with the 1630s ceiling designs for the house. In Campbell's illustration, the sculpture is closer to the building's present appearance. However, we cannot presume from this that the decoration was altered between 1700 and 1717, because the figure sculpture appears to be pre-Restoration in style.

Campbell referred to this building as 'the Grotto', [114] and this designation has continued to be accepted.[165] The façade does not appear in the de Caus views of the garden from either north or south. These show 'the Grotto' as an arcaded structure with three arches to the north and five to the south, but it has been suggested that the pavilion formed an inner façade within 'the Grotto'.[166] De Caus published elevations of the east and west internal walls of the building and it is possible that this façade could have formed the one on the north. It was first identifiably depicted in its location by Stukeley in 1723 who showed it fronting a pavilion to the west of the house at

a Scale of 30 Feet

Extends 52.

The Loggio in the Bowling Green at Wilton.
La Galerie au Jardins.

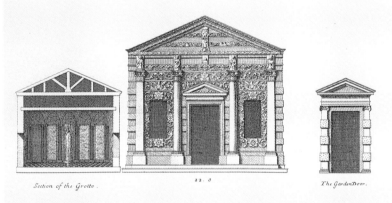

Section of the Grotto.

22. 0

The Garden Door.

Front of the Grotto at Wilton.
Elevation de la Grote.

This Plate is most humbly Inscrib'd to the R.t Hon.ble The Lord Herbert Collonel of his Majesty's Guards,
Lord of the Bed Chamber to his Royal Highness the Prince of Wales &c: and Son and heir to the R.t Hon.ble the Earl of Pembroke &c:

114 The Loggia next to the Bowling Green and the Pavilion, designated 'the Grotto' by Colen Campbell. (*Vitruvius Britannicus*, II, 1717)

115 One of the two columns which originally formed the Coronet Fountains

116 Bridge over the River Wylye, with the statues attributed to Nicholas Stone which were sited in de Caus's garden

the north end of a formal garden of late seventeenth-century appearance.[167]

The pavilion subsequently formed the centrepiece of the arcade at the east end of the newly created lake, which was built in the later 1730s to complement the new Palladian Bridge to the west.[168] By this time its side bays surmounted by volutes had been added.

Stone Columns to the west of the House
These [115] were originally the columns of the Coronet Fountains, which were situated to either side of the central avenue of the garden. According to de Caus, water was forced up 'all theire heigth which causeth the moueing and turning of two Crownes att the top'.[169] The crowns do not survive.

In the early eighteenth century, the columns were sited next to John Webb's gates in the east entrance forecourt.[170]

Marble Statues in the north forecourt
These four figures are shown in the de Caus engraving, set in the middle of the fountains nearest to the house. Lieutenant Hammond provides the identification: 'In one is Venus, with her sonne Cupid in her Armes; in another Diana, with her bathing sheet; in a third is Susanna pulling a thorne out of her Foote; and in the 4th. Cleopatra with the Serpent'.[171] These sculptures are now sited in the garden in the north forecourt. They have been attributed to Nicholas Stone, who is said to have 'desined & built many curious workes for the Earle of Pembroke at his Hons. House at Wilton, near Salsbury & well paide'.[172]

Statues on the Bridge over the River Wylye to the east of the House
These figures, of Flora and Bacchus, possibly also by Stone, were situated originally in the wildernesses in the central part of the de Caus garden. The Bacchus was seen by Defoe inside the house at the foot of the Great Stairs,[173] and both statues were placed in their present position on Westmacott's new bridge in 1826 [116–118].[174]

117 The statue of Flora

118 The statue of Bacchus

119 Westmacott's Loggia in the Italian Garden

120 Relief of Triton
121 Relief of Europa

The Loggia in the Italian Garden
The layout of the Italian Garden to the west of the house was begun in the 1820s, and the Loggia [**119**] was built by Westmacott in 1826.[175] It incorporates four marble bas-reliefs which survive from the de Caus Grotto and were published by him in *Wilton Garden*: two Tritons, Venus and Europa [**120–3**]

The Bronze Gladiator (no longer at Wilton)
De Caus regarded this piece by Hubert le Sueur as a copy of 'the most famous statue of all that antiquity hath left'. The cast was made from Charles I's bronze copy of the Borghese Gladiator, and was placed in the middle of the great oval, the focal point towards the southern end of de Caus's garden. It was presented later by the 8th Earl to Sir Robert Walpole and is now at Houghton.[176] A lead cast was made which remained at Wilton until the early nineteenth century.[177]

Column with Statue of Venus
This is shown by Knyff in the east forecourt. It was taken down during the Wyatt period, and eventually re-erected in its present position to the east of the house in front of an early nineteenth-century three-bay loggia. The antique column of Egyptian granite, from the Temple of Venus Genetrix, was bought by Evelyn for the Arundel collection and was subsequently purchased by the 5th Earl. The capital and base were fitted in the seventeenth century. The Renaissance bronze statue of Venus which surmounts the column was also acquired by Evelyn.[178]

Palladian Bridge
Designed by Roger Morris and the 9th 'Architect' Earl, the bridge [**124,125**] was built in 1736–7 by John Devall the stone-mason, who was paid £103 upon completion.[179] A keystone on the bridge

122 Relief of Triton
123 Relief of Venus

carries the inscription 'JD 1737'. The design was inspired by, but not copied from, Palladio's rejected design for the Rialto Bridge in Venice,[180] and in its turn it inspired imitations at Stowe, Prior Park and Hagley. The River Nadder was dammed below the bridge to form a broad water. At the end of this, a colonnade was constructed, with de Caus's pavilion façade as its centrepiece, from which the bridge could be viewed.

Riding House

Elegant French classical designs for the Riding House were produced in 1755 by Vallin Delamotte for the 10th Earl who was an authority on equitation,[181] and, as designed, the building would not have looked out of place at Versailles. However, it was erected to a far simpler design, and has been altered since. Situated to the north-west of the house, Wyatt used part of it for his kitchen and service range. The interior is now subdivided, but it retains its spectators' gallery.

The present building replaced an earlier riding house which was positioned further to the north of the house.

Archway and Statue of Marcus Aurelius

This full-size replica of the antique Marcus Aurelius was first depicted at Wilton, indistinctly, by Knyff.[182] It is shown clearly in drawings made by Stukeley in 1723, positioned on a triumphal arch on the hill south of the house.[183] The 9th Earl entertained the idea of building a miniature Stonehenge on this hill, based on Stukeley's reconstruction. The Editor of Defoe's *Tour* was enthusiastic: 'it will add to the Curiosities of Wilton; and be the Admiration of Foreigners, as well as Natives: for who, that sees that stupendous Piece of Antiquity in its Ruins, will not be desirous to

124 The Palladian Bridge:
view from the west

125 The Palladian Bridge:
view from the north

behold it, as it was in its supposed flourishing State?'[184]

The 10th Earl did not take up his father's idea. The Marcus Aurelius was reset, in the position shown by Stukeley [**126**], on a new stone archway designed by Sir William Chambers *c.* 1759 [**127**], who referred to it as 'the first work of stone I executed in England'.[185]

Wyatt brought the arch and statue down to the north forecourt to provide his new entrance gateway [**128**], and added the flanking lodges. This would have pleased Gilpin, who regarded the placing of the arch on top of the hill as an absurdity: 'A triumphal arch would be perhaps too pompous a structure to form a part of the approach to the house; yet in that capacity it might have been suffered; it might have had some analogy at least to its situation. But as it now stands, however good it may be in itself, it is certainly an absurd ostentatious ornament'.[186] The Marcus Aurelius statue is apparently of lead, coloured to resemble bronze.[187]

Lord Pembrokes Garden at Wilton 20. Aug.

A. Sr Philip Sidneys Walk.

The Casino

This small tetrastyle doric temple, was built by Sir William Chambers *c.* 1759 as an eyecatcher on the hill to the south of the stables [129].[188]

Well-head in the central courtyard

The octagonal Venetian or Longobardic well-head in the courtyard [130,131] replaces the fountain which is shown on Colen Campbell's plan.[189] There was a brisk export trade in well-heads from Venice in the nineteenth century, and the Wilton example was presumably acquired at that time. Well-heads are difficult to date because of their general absence of inscriptions, and because of the conservatism of the form. Also, it must be noted that a number of fakes were put on to the market when the trade was at its height.[190] However, despite these caveats, the Wilton well-head appears from its vocabulary of patterned ornament to be datable to the ninth or tenth century.[191] It is perhaps unusual for Venice, where the favoured form was the

126 William Stukeley's view of the garden from the house, made in 1723, which shows the statue of Marcus Aurelius on an archway to the south of the house. (Bodleian Library, Ms Top Gen d 13, fo 10r)

127 Sir William Chambers' arch and the statue of Marcus Aurelius, seen from the entrance forecourt

128 The entrance to Wilton House: the arch and statue, and Wyatt's lodges, seen from the north

129 Sir William Chambers' Casino, on the hill to the south of the house

130 The octagonal well-head in the central courtyard: *see also* **86**

131 The well-head: detail of the decorative carving

cylinder or capital rather than the octagon.[192]

Park Wall

The parkland to the south of the house was once traversed by a public road running from Netherhampton to Bulbridge, passing by Washern Grange.

During the mid sixteenth century it was diverted further south, and part of the area, then known as 'Rowlington Park', was enclosed late in the same century by a brick and stone boundary wall on the east, west and south sides, of which most of the south and west sides remain.[193] The erection of this wall is attributed to Adrian Gilbert, a 'great Chymist', but 'the greatest Buffoon in the Nation', half-brother to Sir Walter Raleigh and 'laborator' to the Countess of Pembroke.[194]

The road from Quidhampton to Wilton town, which passed close to the east front of the house, was diverted to join the Salisbury to Bath turnpike *c.* 1805. At this time the park boundary was moved to the east to adjoin the new road. In 1826–7 Gilbert's now redundant eastern boundary wall was demolished, and a new wall of yellow brick was built alongside the new road.[195] This new wall, over 2,300 yards long, extends around the north side of the garden as well. The materials from Gilbert's old wall were re-used, extending his surviving south and west walls, to enclose the area known as 'shoulder of mutton corner'.

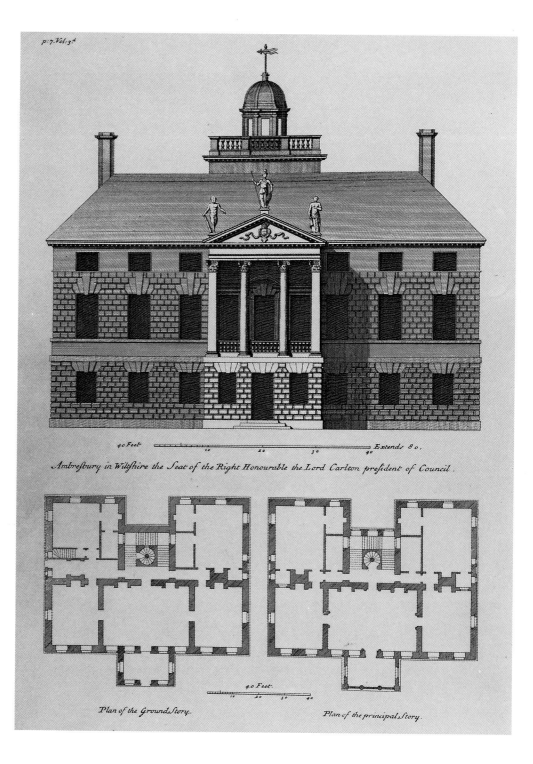

40 Feet   10   20   30   40   Extends 8 0.

Ambresbury in Wiltshire the Seat of the Right Honourable the Lord Carlton president of Council.

40 Feet   10   20   30   40

Plan of the Ground Story.   *Plan of the principal Story.*

132 South elevation and plans of ground and first floors. (Colen Campbell, *Vitruvius Britannicus*, III, 1725)

Amesbury Abbey

Ownership and Outline History

In recounting the origins of the priory at Amesbury Sir Richard Colt Hoare tells us that two nunneries of the Benedictine order were founded by Queen Aelfthryth in the late tenth century as penance for her part in the murder of her stepson, Edward the Martyr, at Corfe.[1] One was at Amesbury, the other at Wherwell in Hampshire. The house at Amesbury was dissolved by Henry II in 1177, and refounded by him nine years later as a priory attached to the Abbey of Fontevrault. At the Dissolution, the buildings and lands were surrendered to the Crown by the Abbess, Joan Darell.[2]

Following the birth of a son to Henry VIII and Jane Seymour in 1537, Sir Edward Seymour, Baron Beauchamp, brother to the Queen, was created Earl of Hertford and received a grant of the Amesbury Abbey estates. From 1541 to 1543 the buildings were partially demolished and the materials sold, those 'to remayn undefaced' being 'the lodging called the Priore's Lodging . . . the long stable with the hay barne adjoining, the whete barn, the baking house and the gate with the gate-house in the base court'. Rooms in the 'Priore's Lodging' were prepared for the Earl when he visited his property in 1543.[3]

After the death of Henry VIII in 1547, Hertford, uncle to the boy king, Edward VI, was chosen by his fellow members of the governing council as Protector of the Realm and Governor of the King's Person. Six weeks later, as Duke of Somerset, he had himself appointed Protector by patent and was thus vested with as much authority as any could wield, short of wearing the crown. Protector Somerset customarily enters histories of architecture as the moving force behind the building of the innovative Somerset House in the Strand, but he did not long enjoy the fruits of his enlightened patronage, nor did he have the opportunity to build a new palace in Wiltshire. He was accused of treason, attainted, his honours forfeit, and brought to the block in 1552.

The Protector's son, Edward Seymour, was later restored to favour by Elizabeth I as Baron Beauchamp and Earl of Hertford, and he regained the property at Amesbury. This he leased in 1560 to his steward, John Barwycke of Wilcot, the house at this time being said to be 'in great ruin', but the Earl promised to repair it. By 1595, Barwycke's widow, Dorothy, had sub-let the property to Philip Poore of the George Inn, Amesbury, also a Seymour tenant.[4] Shortly after this, two new lodges were built on the eastern boundary of the park: 'Diana her hous', dated 1600 and Kent House, 1607.

Edward, Earl of Hertford, like his father before him, was deprived of his titles, having married without permission the Queen's cousin, Lady Catherine Grey, the repudiated wife of Henry, Lord Herbert, later 2nd Earl of Pembroke, but he was subsequently restored to honour as 1st Earl of Hertford.[5] He continued to lease the properties at Amesbury, giving William Allen of Amesbury, innholder, the tenure of the George Inn, and also 'the site of the late Priory of Amesbury with capital mansion house of late erected by the Earl on a parcel of his farm', including 'the gatehouse near the George Inn, and all outhouses, kitchens, laundryes, brewhouses, slaughter-houses, stables, barns, coach houses . . .'[6]

The 1st Earl was succeeded by his grandson, William. He too had made an injudicious, possibly unlawful, marriage with Lady Arabella Stuart, the niece of Lord Darnley, thus presenting a possible threat to the succession, but after a period in exile he was restored to royal favour and was created Marquess of Hertford in 1640. After his subsequent distinguished conduct for the Royalist cause in the Civil War, he was restored to the Dukedom of Somerset by Act of Parliament on 13 September 1660. He died shortly after, on 24 October. His eldest son having predeceased him, the title passed to his grandson, William, who was only eight years old.

The Seymour property had been seized for the State during the Interregnum and the 'Abbey Ground and Park' tenanted by Thomas Gray of Amesbury.[7] The Marquess himself appears to have been allowed to keep the buildings for his own residence, and it was perhaps in antici-pation of a happy Restoration, coupled with a desire to provide a suitable seat for his grandson, that he employed John Webb to design a house to replace the one which his own grandfather had rebuilt or repaired.

Webb's Amesbury was designed before 1660 and built on the site of the older priory. The Marquess's death, occurring so soon after his restoration to the Dukedom of Somerset, left his widow in some financial confusion. In letters written in 1664 she refers to debts 'whereof there hath beene no interest paid since the Duke's death', and to 'moneys owing to the workmen for the building at Amsbury'. She feared that land would have to be sold to clear these commitments.[8] The young William died, unmarried, in 1671 and four years later his uncle and successor, John, the 4th Duke, died without male issue. At this point the Marquessate of Hertford became extinct and the Dukedom of Somerset devolved upon the 4th Duke's cousin Francis Seymour. In 1676, John's niece, Elizabeth, by marriage to Thomas, 2nd Earl of Ailesbury, carried the Ames-bury estate and the other Seymour prop-erties of Savernake and Tottenham Park, into the family of Bruce. In 1686 Ames-bury was leased to Viscount Shannon, a distant cousin of Thomas Bruce, and in 1708 Lord Bruce, heir apparent of the Earl of Ailesbury, leased it to William Benson of Bromley, Middlesex, who shortly embarked upon the building of Wilbury, five miles away, a house based closely upon Amesbury. Amesbury was sub-sequently owned, from 1720 until his death in 1725, by Henry Boyle, Lord Carleton, Chancellor of the Exchequer and Principal Secretary of State in the reign of Queen Anne, a grandson of both John, the 4th Duke of Somerset and Richard, the 1st Earl of Burlington.

Carleton bequeathed the house and estate to Charles Douglas, 3rd Duke of Queensberry, a cousin of the Earl of Ailesbury. He had enlargements carried out by Henry Flitcroft, an appointment presumably made upon the advice of another cousin, Richard, the 3rd Earl of Burlington. He also employed Charles Bridgeman to landscape the gardens. Queensberry outlived his sons and was succeeded in 1778 by his cousin William, who is said to have taken fittings and pictures from Amesbury for his villa at Richmond.[9] From 1792 to 1794 the house was again leased, to Sir Elijah Impey, and was then the refuge for five years for a community of English nuns, canonesses of St Augustine, who had been expelled from Louvain.

Notwithstanding his taking of the title Baron Douglas of Amesbury in 1786, William, 4th Duke of Queensberry and 3rd Earl of March, seldom visited the house and upon his dying unmarried in 1810, the estate devolved to Archibald, Lord Douglas of Douglas. It was offered for sale, being bought eventually in 1824 for £145,000 by Sir Edmund Antrobus, 1st Baronet, of Cheshire.[10] He died within two years, and his nephew and heir, Sir Edmund William Antrobus, after first employing J H Flooks of Wilton to make estimates for alterations, then turned to the fashionable country house architect, Thomas Hopper, who performed the grandiose rebuilding of the Webb house. Further works were carried out in 1904 by Detmar Blow.

Amesbury remained the property of the Antrobus family until 1979, its interior in recent years being subdivided to form flats. By 1981 it had been converted into a residential nursing-home.

The House *c.* 1660

Amesbury has been justly described as John Webb's 'triumph in country house design'.[11] Themes adumbrated at the architect's slightly earlier Gunnersbury House are here brought to fruition, in an ensemble whose 'uncommon grandeur', C R Cockerell tells us, 'fills and occupies the mind'. Cockerell, visiting the house in 1823, recognised the triumph but not its author, supposing the design to be by Inigo Jones, his genius being 'in few examples more conspicuous'.[12] In this supposition he followed Colen Campbell and George Vertue, both of whom tended to conflate the work of Jones with that of Webb, and thus considered, as the house was built after the death of the

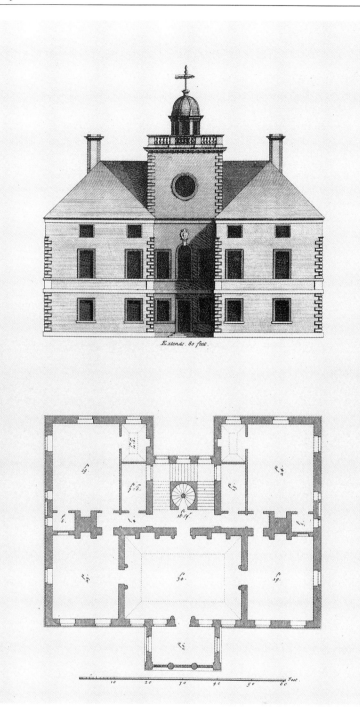

133 The north front and first-floor plan. (William Kent, *Designs of Inigo Jones*, 1727)

134 The south elevation with the eighteenth-century wings, drawn by Wyatt Papworth. (RIBA Drawings Collection)

135 First-floor plan, drawn by Wyatt Papworth. Papworth, unlike Campbell and Kent, depicts the central stair in the newel of the main stair correctly, as oval. (RIBA Drawings Collection)

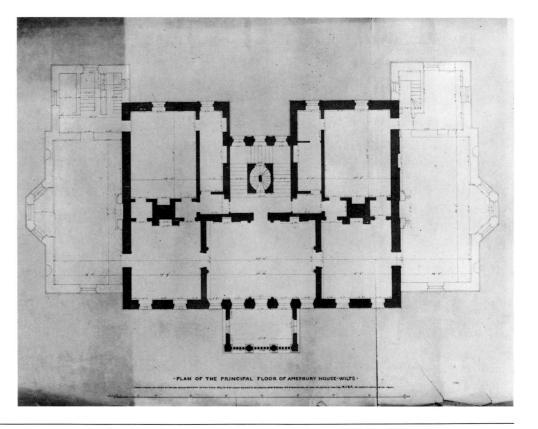

Surveyor, that Webb was merely realising his master's Idea.[13]

Amesbury is recorded for us not only by Cockerell's sketches and notes, but also by the engravings in Campbell's *Vitruvius Britannicus* (1725) [132] and Kent's *Designs of Inigo Jones* [133] (1727; after drawings by Flitcroft). A series of invaluable sketches made by C J Richardson in 1817 and 1829[14] provided the basis for Wyatt Papworth's presentation drawings of 1840–1 [134,135],[15] and further evidence for the appearance of the house, before the employment of Hopper, is provided by Flooks' plans of 1831.[16] In addition, William Stukeley in 1740 published a distant view of the house from the north [136],[17] and engraved views from the south were published in 1787 by Harrison,[18] and in 1826 by Colt Hoare, the latter after a drawing by Buckler of 1805.[19]

136 William Stukeley's *Prospect of Vespasians Camp near Ambsbury*, drawn in 1723, which depicts the house from the north. Stukeley published the view in 1740. (Godfrey Meynell Collection, Meynell Langley, Derbyshire)

137 John Webb, design for a composite capital depicting the Seymour phoenix in flames. (Devonshire Collection, Chatsworth)

138 Cartouche displaying achievements of the Somerset arms: formerly set in the pediment of the south front

139 Cartouche, formerly set on the north front above the central first-floor window

Only one of John Webb's drawings for the house survives.[20] Inscribed 'Ambresbury for Marquisse Hertford', it depicts a composite capital (for the portico or the saloon) in which the phoenix in flames, emblematic of the Seymours, is set between acanthus leaves [137]. That the patron is referred to as Hertford rather than Somerset indicates that the design was made before the restoration of the Dukedom in September 1660. It is unlikely that Webb would have turned to the design of such a detail as this before it was necessary, so we might surmise that the building programme had been under way for at least a year by the time of the full restitution of the family honours.

The family is also commemorated in the cartouches which were placed originally on the south and north fronts of the house [138,139]. Both of these, achievements of the Somerset arms, survive in the porte-cochère of the present mansion. They display shields bearing the six principal quarterings of Seymour. The one from the pediment, originally ensigned by a ducal coronet, has its quarterings enclosed within a garter, which confirms the 2nd Duke as builder of the house: he had been nomi-

nated KG at Jersey in 1649/50, and invested at Canterbury in May 1660, but never installed. The second cartouche, from above the central first-floor window on the north front, also displays the Seymour quarterings but without the garter.[21]

It has been suggested by Sir John Summerson[22] that Amesbury is an elaboration of an early Palladio design, the Villa Godi at Lonedo.[23] Indeed, we find there a comparable symmetry about a central axis and an elevation which might have provided a model for the rear of Amesbury.[24] However, the front elevation of Amesbury appears to be in the line of descent from Inigo Jones's Prince's Lodging at Newmarket;[25] and in plan the house has a greater subtlety and degree of integration in its elements than the Villa Godi [141] and might be seen as a development from Webb's own Gunnersbury House,[26] a design which owes far more to Palladio and to Inigo Jones in its compartmenting of space than does Amesbury. One of the closest parallels to the Amesbury plan is in fact provided by a later Palladian, Francesco Muttoni, whose design of 1706 for the Palazzetto Maioli at Vicenza, in a manner similar to Webb but half a century later,

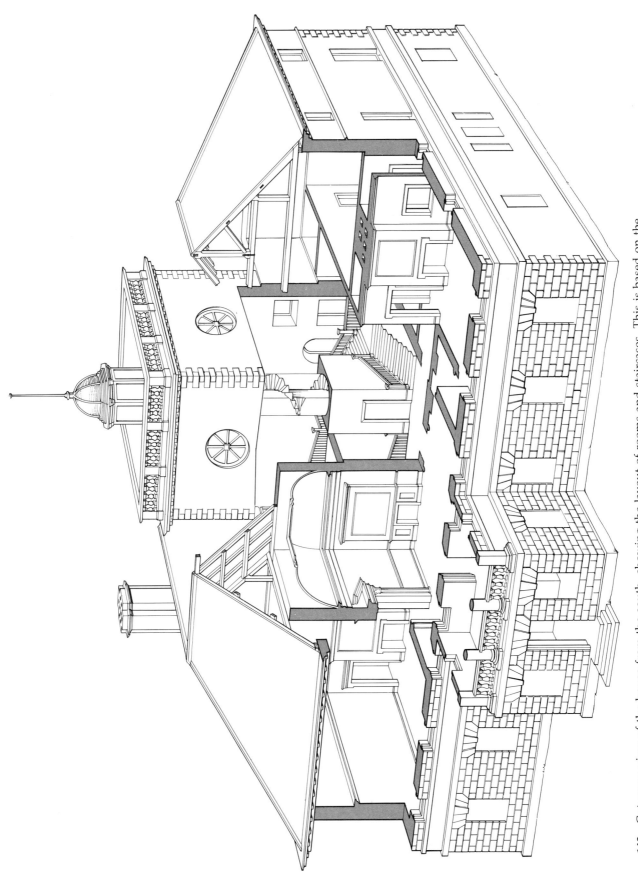

140 Cut-away view of the house from the south, showing the layout of rooms and staircases. This is based on the Wyatt Papworth and J H Flooks drawings. The roof structure is conjectural

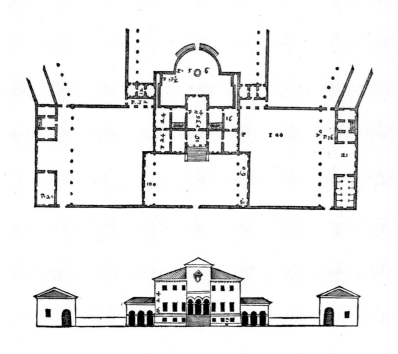

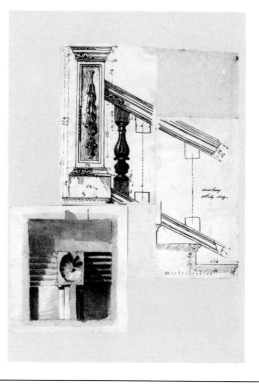

141 A Palladio, the Villa Godi. (*I Quattro Libri dell'Architettura*, II, 1570)

142 The staircase, drawn by C J Richardson in 1829. (Metropolitan Museum of Art, New York; Harris Brisbane Dick Fund 1926, 26.85, 236v)

effects a like balance between separation and communication.[27] At Gunnersbury, Webb had provided discrete clusters of interconnecting rooms separated by grand, formal, central, spaces. Amesbury is smaller and tauter, retaining the idea of interconnecting rooms, but linking them also by a central corridor [140]. It was the planning of Amesbury which drew the highest praise from Cockerell:

> Plan regular and remarkably elegant. Saloon above stairs delightful with handsome dressings to doors, chimney pieces and ceilings – contrivance of the staircase with backstairs in the newel the most convenient and elegant that can be conceived . . . There are offices below as well as abundant bed Ro: above & I consider that for economy of convenience with proportion & effect, it may challenge any Ho: in England ancient or modern.[28]

The staircase arrangement had previously inspired both Sir William Chambers and James Paine to the sincerest form of flattery, Chambers copying the idea for Lord Bessborough's villa at Roehampton,[29] and Paine, who had made plans of Amesbury, employing it in his design for Belford Hall, Northumberland.[30]

The main stair, as Cockerell noted and as Flooks' drawings confirm, rose through two storeys to the chamber floor, whilst the central stair, which was oval [142], not round as depicted by Campbell and Kent, carried on to the cupola.[13] The genesis of this invention is not clear cut. Webb might have derived it from his copy of Serlio, where a similar arrangement is indicated in a design for an astylar house in *Book VII*.[32] The idea occurs again in the Palazzo del Babilano Pallavicino [143], published in another book available to Webb, Rubens' *Palazzi di Genova* of 1622. The arrangement can also be seen as part of the wholly English development of walling-in the core of an open-well stair to provide storage space. It is a short step, technically if not conceptually, from using the central space as cupboards to using it for a secondary stair.[33] Lastly, we might look to the corpus of ideas embodied for us in the drawings of John Thorpe. Thorpe's plan of Sir Thomas Darrell's house shows a staircase of three flights, ascending around an open well, without a central newel stair, but placed in the same way as Webb's at the centre of the rear of the house between two slightly projecting wings.[34]

The positioning of the stairs appears to have been Webb's starting-point in his planning of the house. The neatness of this contrivance, allied with the provision of the corridor, enabled him to make the rear rooms especially usable as self-contained apartments, comprising bedrooms and accompanying dressing-rooms, separate from the formal sequence of hall, main stair, saloon and portico. The saloon, as Papworth's drawing shows [**144**], achieved grandeur despite its relatively modest size, its coved ceiling, accommodated within the chamber storey, recalling the Cube Rooms at Wilton, not only in architectural form but also in the nature of the painted decoration of the coving.

Cockerell's only caveats in his extended praise of Amesbury come in his description of the outside: 'The whole exterior from the high plinth of the roof, dormers in the roof, & crowded windows is not very agreable in point of

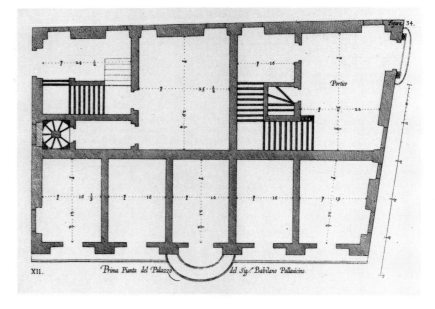

proportion', but on the other hand, 'the tower ... corresponding chimney shafts, & projection of the Portico is of the best school & contrivance'. Similarly, although the 'keystones are heavy & the corinthian order is grosso', it is nonetheless 'elegantly conceived and placed'.

The criticism of the windows is pertinent. The dormers did clutter the roofline, but although probable it is not certain whether they were original, or whether the attic floor was inserted in the eighteenth century to increase the

143 Plan of the Palazzo del Babilano Pallavicino: the staircase arrangement might have influenced Webb's design. (P P Rubens, *Palazzi di Genova*, 1622)

144 Cross-section through the first-floor rooms of Webb's house, drawn by Wyatt Papworth. (RIBA Drawings Collection)

·SECTION·OF·THE·PRINCIPAL·APARTMENTS·OF·AMESBURY·HOUSE·WILTS·

145 The north front, drawn by C J Richardson in 1817. (Metropolitan Museum of Art, New York; Harris Brisbane Dick Fund 1926, 26.85, 239v)

146 The heavy keystone over the first-floor door on to the portico, rebuilt by Hopper, closely following Webb's original

accommodation. Access to it was gained by short flights of stairs situated to either side of the central stair tower.[35] The omission of the dormers by Campbell and Kent in their illustrations is not conclusive evidence: they might well have found them inappropriate in a canonical Palladian design. Kent was inaccurate elsewhere: in the pursuit of symmetry he adjusted the illustration of the rear of the house, placing the back door in an implausible central position where the stair would have cut across. Richardson's sketch [145] shows it to one side, below the second landing from whence it would have provided direct access beneath the third flight to the central passage.

The crowded windows and first-floor door on to the portico, topped by dramatically heavy keystones [146], appear again on Webb's King Charles Building at Greenwich, and the precisely cut rustication, alternating with plain bands of ashlar made this a bustling façade which was successfully resolved visually by the very neat portico. Webb's portico at Gunnersbury was criticised by Sir Roger Pratt[36] and later Roger North,[37] on the grounds of the climate and the limiting of the daylight which entered the house, but he was keen to design them, despite the vagaries of the English

weather. He had built the first projecting temple front on an English country house, at The Vyne in Hampshire [147], and had proposed a portico for Lamport[38] and also probably for Syon.[39] He had succeeded in building one at Gunnersbury but there it was *in antis*. At Amesbury it projected. In designing porticoes, Webb was very consciously following the wishful thinking of Palladio, who argued that porticoes were built on ancient temples after the model of private houses. Having found an absence of the form in his copy of Serlio, Webb conceded to himself that 'it may bee the Ancients did not use them but in Temples and Publique works . . .'[40] but he remained an enthusiast.

Kent's illustration of the rear of the house, rather more than Richardson's sketch, suggests further Palladian inspiration. The singularly cubic arrangement of masses and the staccato rhythm of the windows takes us back to the illustration of the Villa Godi in the *Quattro Libri*. But to gain this effect Kent has adjusted the proportions, lowered the tower and omitted the upper windows of the main stair. As a further concession to Palladian taste, both he and Campbell omitted the emblematic details from the composite capitals in their illustrations of the entrance front.

147 The Vyne, Sherborne St John, Hampshire: the temple front portico added to the house by John Webb *c.* 1654 to *c.* 1656

148 Henry Flitcroft's survey of the Amesbury estate, 1726: detail showing the house and grounds. (WRO 944/1)

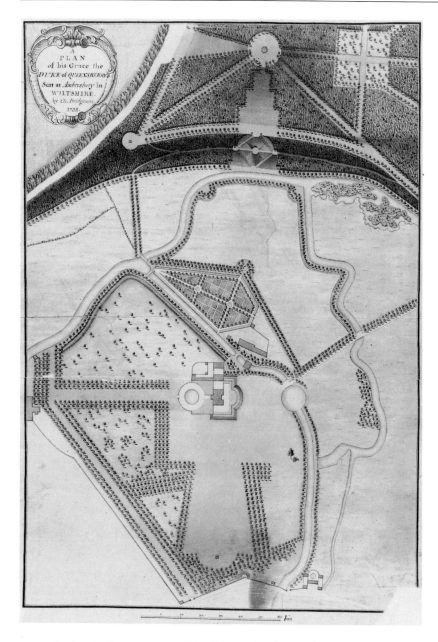

149 Charles Bridgeman's plan of the estate, 1738. (Bodleian Library, Ms Gough Drawing a 3*)

The House in the Eighteenth Century

The Duke and Duchess of Queensberry were members of Lord Burlington's circle in the early 1720s, so it is no surprise to find them taking a house designed by Leoni on the newly laid-out Burlington estate in London in 1722 and employing Henry Flitcroft, a Burlington protégé, to produce a survey of their new estate at Amesbury in 1726 [148][41]. Regular payments were made thereafter to Flitcroft by the Duke for a period of well over

thirty years,[42] a good deal of the money presumably being spent at Amesbury, to which the Queensberrys retired in 1729, following their championing of their old friend, John Gay, whose controversial opera, *Polly*, had incurred the displeasure of the Lord Chamberlain and the Court.[43]

Sir John Clerk of Penicuik, visiting Amesbury in 1727 had found 'no great matter in it', the 'high drawing room' being the only good one in the house and the roofs being too low.[44] The Queensberrys however did not improve the house immediately, but turned their attention first to the grounds. In 1731 the Duchess had countered Swift's suggestion that, while the park at Amesbury was pleasant enough, the house was too small, with the assertion that 'the house is big enough but the Parke is too little'.[45] Purchase of land to the north of the River Avon, which had previously bounded the estate, and of 'Vespasian's Camp', the Iron Age hill-fort to the west, rectified the situation, the latter providing the natural focus for the new landscape layout for which Bridgeman produced a plan in 1738 [149].[46] In a further letter to Swift, in May 1733, the Duchess wrote that 'his Grace & I have been here this fortnight with no other Company than Bricklayers and labourers, we are throwing down a parcel of walls that block'd us up every way, and making a sunk fence round the house'.[47] Comparison of the Flitcroft and Bridgeman surveys reveals the extent of this work. The walls enclosed formal gardens to the north and north-east of the house; these were replaced by the ha-ha.

Work on the landscape continued for several years after, note being made in the 1748 edition of Defoe's *Tour* that, although the house was 'not much to be admired', 'the present Duke has made great improvements in his gardens; having inclosed and planted a large steep hill; at the foot of which the River Avon very beautifully winds, as also through the greatest part of the garden . . . When the whole of the Duke's design is

150 J Buckler's drawing of the house in 1805, published by R Colt Hoare in 1826. (WAS, Devizes)

151 Amesbury in 1787, after the addition of the wings, illustrated by Harrison and Co (*Picturesque Views of the Principal Seats*)

completed it will not be inferior to any of the finest Places in these Parts'.[48] These points were made again in later editions. The editor had not kept abreast of developments, for work certainly had begun on improving the house in 1750, and the wings are shown clearly on Andrews' and Dury's map of 1773.[49]

Mrs Montagu, visiting the house twenty years after Sir John Clerk, made similar criticisms, noting that although 'the front looks very prettily on the outside', 'within there are but few rooms, only one good one and that is regular and is prettily furnished with Mr Wootton's landscapes'.[50] Wootton was a friend of John Gay and thus an obvious artist for the Queensberrys to patronise.[51] His Claudian scenes are depicted by Papworth in his section through the Webb saloon. No reference is made either by Mrs Montagu or elsewhere to the decorations by Thornhill for which oil sketches were made: the *Seasons & Cupid* and *Mercury & Hymen*. Either these have been destroyed or they were not executed.[52]

Three years after Mrs Montagu's visit, the Reverend Richard Woodyeare was able to describe (in 1750) 'a grand new Room and furniture, Chimneypieces, red and white marble: the fable of the Stork and the Fox carved on them: Emblems of Her Grace's hospitality'.[53] He was probably referring to the first-floor drawing-room in the new east wing, which in addition to the chimney-piece was distinguished by a coved ceiling. Work on the west wing was not completed until several years later. It was still proceeding in 1757, when nine loads of Chilmark stone were brought,[54] and between 1756 and 1761 William Privett, the local mason, was in receipt of nearly £350, probably in payment for this work.[55]

The attribution of the wings to Flitcroft is based not on direct references or drawings, but on the circumstantial evidence provided by the regular payments and on the Burlington–Queensberry connection. They can also be attributed on stylistic

grounds. Flanking the Webb house, set back slightly from the plane of the entrance front, they have the unobtrusive air of the mid eighteenth-century small villa and an economy of detail which suggests considerable empathy with the original building. The towers to the rear of each wing recall Burlington's flanking towers at Tottenham Park, and so by extension the towers at Wilton. They also gracefully echo Webb's stair tower by including round windows in their upper sections.

Each wing contained a large first-floor room: the drawing-room to the east and the dining-room to the west. Both had central fireplaces opposite canted bay windows. Below the dining-room Flitcroft built a new two-storey kitchen. In a note of November 1778, one month after the death of the 3rd Duke, it was suggested that this should be converted into a servants' hall and is referred to as such on Flooks' plans, although confusingly, it is still referred to as a kitchen on Cockerell's plan.[56] Under the drawing-room Flitcroft placed a library. The new west wing was cellared, linking up with the cellars which stretched along the south and west ranges of the original house. The 1778 note refers also to the construction of a cantilevered balcony 2'6'' deep around the octagonal bow of the dining-room. This is visible on the engraving of 1826 [**150**].

Further piecemeal work to be carried out by one George Parsons of Amesbury was ordered by the 4th Duke in 1781. As well as making the doors 'to go easy', this included placing chimneys in each of the tower rooms, and fitting sash windows in the garrets.[57]

Following the major extensions to the Webb house, Harrison's description of 1787 [**151**] marks a welcome change from those which have gone before: the apartments are now 'numerous and superb' and 'all richly furnished and many of them fitted up in a splendid modern stile, by the late Duke'.[58]

Full-time occupation of the house by the Queensberrys ceased with the death

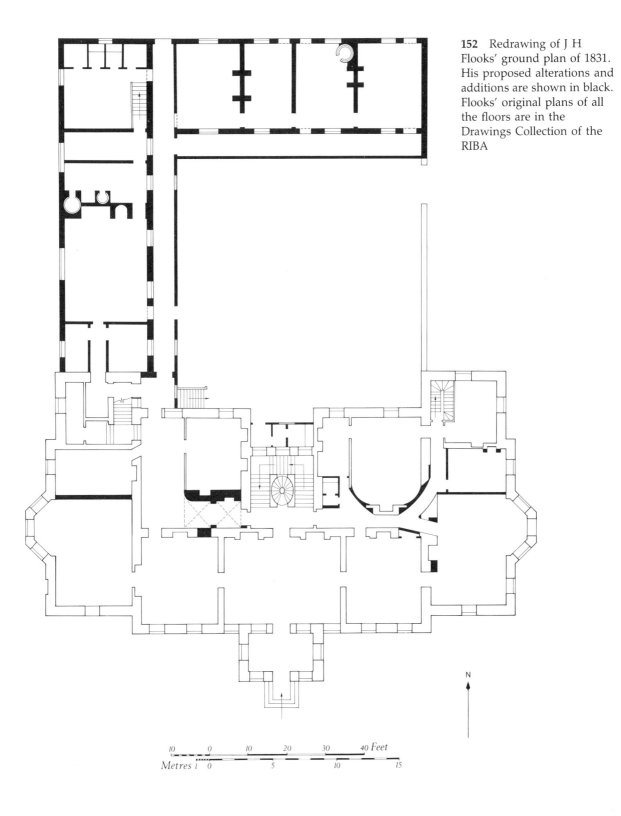

152 Redrawing of J H Flooks' ground plan of 1831. His proposed alterations and additions are shown in black. Flooks' original plans of all the floors are in the Drawings Collection of the RIBA

N

10 0 10 20 30 40 *Feet*

Metres 1 0 5 10 15

of the 3rd Duke in 1778, although the 4th Duke must have been at least an occasional user of his property to justify the alterations which he proposed in the early years of his ownership. In 1801 John Britton found the estate overgrown[59] and the picturesqueness of such decay clearly appealed to the Prince de Condé and the Duc de Bourbon, who visited with the intention of renting Amesbury as a summer residence. They were apparently delighted with both the house and grounds but found that it was not furnished as they had expected, the furnishings having been taken away by the 4th Duke.[60]

No description of the house is given in the sales particulars of 1824.[61] Reference is made to the whole of the estate except the mansion being let at 'very moderate Rents', and to the existence of offices, stables and coach yard. The offices were apparently capable of improvement, for when John Harris Flooks of Wilton submitted his plans for alterations in 1831, these included substantial service wings to the north, forming two sides of a walled courtyard [152]. His proposals inside the house were largely concerned with the improvement of lines of communication, not without considerable detriment to Webb's north side first-floor rooms, which were to be reduced to permit the construction of a corridor running from wing to wing. New corridors were also proposed on the ground and second floors but the changes involved would have been less sweeping.

Flooks' incidental naming of several of the rooms on his plans provides the evidence for one important change in the accommodation which had occurred since Flitcroft's time: the moving of the main family bedrooms and dressing-rooms from the first floor to the second where they were situated on the west side adjacent to the nursery.

It does not appear that any of Flooks' proposals were carried out and, following the discovery of dry rot, a radical rebuilding was begun in 1834 to the designs of Thomas Hopper.[62]

The Nineteenth-Century House

The Amesbury Abbey which we see today is substantially the creation of Thomas Hopper, an architect recently characterised as a 'thoroughgoing eclectic', whose buildings 'reflect most of the architectual fashions of the late Georgian period'.[63] His rebuilding of the house incorporated some of the original walls and some eighteenth-century fittings [153]. The rhetorical late Palladian style of the whole, despite the considerable increase in both size and scale, was clearly intended further to reflect Webb's design [154].

Measurements of the present house indicate that the Flitcroft additions were swept away and the original portico demolished, but that the lower storeys of Webb's south front, the return walls in the cellar and some internal walls survive. The cellars under the southern parts of the house remain, reconstructed in the nineteenth century with round-arched brick vaulting, but retaining an original seventeenth-century chamfered door surround [155] to the west side underneath the hall. A seventeenth-century bolection-moulded chimney-piece [156] also survives in the west side ground-floor drawing-room.

Hopper considerably extended in depth the original rectangle defined by Webb, added a larger, hexastyle portico to the south, and projecting Cockerellian porticoes with three-quarter giant columns to the east and west [157]. He also increased the height of the house, making the original chamber floor into a storey of full height. Much of the original masonry of the two lower storeys on the south front survives, excepting the three central bays on the first floor. The original masonry can be distinguished from that of 1834 by the variations in the jointing of the rustication.

Hopper's rebuilding also followed the original scheme in placing the main rooms in a *piano nobile* raised above a low ground storey. The main staircase [159] built immediately to the north of the site

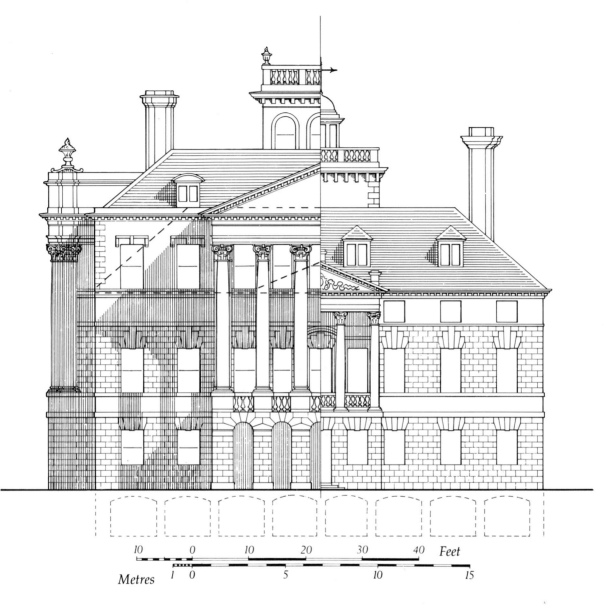

10   0   10   20   30   40 *Feet*

Metres 1   0   5   10   15

of Webb's stair rose to the first floor only. It was treated by Hopper almost as an apartment in its own right, being built on a spectacular scale, top-lit and massively arcaded with Vanbrughian galleries [158] which were perhaps inspired by Kings Weston, the house of a former patron of Hopper, P J Miles. Before the subdivision of the house into flats, the first-floor gallery provided access to three large rooms: the east side drawing-room [160], which retains the chimney-piece re-marked by the Reverend Woodyeare, and the west side dining-room both 36'

by 24'; and the enormous saloon (74' by 22') [162] which occupied the whole of the south front and gave on to the balcony of the porte-cochère. The upper storeys are reached by a secondary stair [161], with a scrolled, wrought-iron balustrade, which rises behind the main stair from ground floor to attic. The rear of the house comprises the service range which was extended in 1860.

The service block has been altered internally since completion, most particu-larly in recent years, but a reconstruction of its original appearance may be

153 Comparative drawing, showing the Webb and Hopper houses

154 (above)   Hopper's
Amesbury, from the south

155 (right)   An original
seventeenth-century
chamfered door surround in
the reconstructed cellars

156 (far right)   A
seventeenth-century
chimney-piece in the
ground-floor drawing-room

attempted [**163**].[64] It is of three storeys, with access to the main body of the house originally at ground-floor level only. On the first-floor east side, a large self-contained room, possibly for the accommodation of the cook, was reached by a staircase from the kitchen below.[65] Two further stairs, placed side by side in the centre of the range, rose from the ground to the second floor. The westernmost of these, the only one of the three staircases in the service block to survive, gave access to both the first and second-floor servants' rooms. The eastern did not, being built to provide access directly from the ground floor working areas to the servants' bedrooms on the upper floor, above the suggested cook's room. Such a proliferation of staircases within a small space provides an illuminating illustration of the principles of separation of both people and functions, stated initially in the writings of Pratt and North in the seventeenth century, and firmly established in house-planning by the mid nineteenth century.[66] As Jane Austen's Catherine Morland had discovered to her cost, routes could be prescribed or proscribed in both the public and private parts of the country house.[67]

Access from the service range to the rest of the house at Amesbury is now possible at first-floor level as well as at ground level. A door has been inserted to the east of the open well, and in the well itself a two-storey corridor was inserted on the west side *c.* 1900 to provide an additional linking route. Access between the house and services at second-floor level is not possible because of the considerable difference in floor levels.

157 The rebuilt and extended Amesbury, from the west

158 (above left)   The top-lit, galleried stairwell

159 (below left)   The principal stairs

160 (above right)   Drawing-room on the first floor with the eighteenth-century chimney-piece

161 (below right)   The secondary stairs

At the time of Hopper's death in 1856, the main part of the house still had not been completed, apparently. Work on it is said to have stopped for a few years and was not resumed until 1857.[68]

During the work on Hopper's building, tile paving was uncovered beneath the service buildings just to the north of the Webb house. In 1860, the excavation of trenches for the additional

buildings revealed 'the perfect floors of several apartments' which 'still lay buried at a depth of from three to four feet below the surface of the ground'.[69] The finding of these thirteenth-century tiled floors confirmed that the Webb house had been built partly on the site of the original monastic building.

It is of incidental interest that Hopper, as befitted a successful and fashionable

architect, made full use of the newly available products of industry, using steel beams in the ceiling of the porte-cochère and fitting plate-glass windows. These windows in particular underline how far Hopper's conception was from the seventeenth century, and how far he restated Webb's theme in more ponderous terms.

Some of the work which has been presumed hitherto to be by Hopper was carried out by the prolific Detmar Blow in 1904.[70] He was at pains to copy his predecessor wherever possible, noting on one of his drawings: 'All details marked like this are existing and must be used again – the remaining should be cast in plaster from them'. This fidelity and the later alterations to the house have contributed to the concealment of his efforts.

Blow's drawings testify to his responsibility for works in the entrance hall, which he paved, the stairwell [164], and the long saloon [165]. A drawing [166] made in 1885 by J J Cole shows that Hopper's staircase originally rose in three short flights to the first floor around a square well, before giving on to the south corridor.[71] Blow replaced this with a single, straight flight to the north side corridor, an arrangement which ironically is very similar to Hopper's pre-Amesbury staircase at Melford.[72] He also remade the octagonal skylight, following Hopper, but using a simpler key pattern in the decorative surround.

In the saloon, or morning-room, later known as the ballroom or music room, Blow was responsible for a general refitting. Hopper's tripartite division of the room, defined by pilasters carrying beams, was retained, but Blow substituted coupled, fluted half-columns, and replaced the original flat ceiling with a shallow cove. He also blocked two of the room's three fireplaces, retaining only the central one, which he fitted with a new chimney-piece flanked by coupled, fluted columns of the same composite order as the coupled columns which articulated the walls. This fireplace was itself blocked, and the chimney-piece removed, when a wall was erected at this point during the conversion of the house into flats.

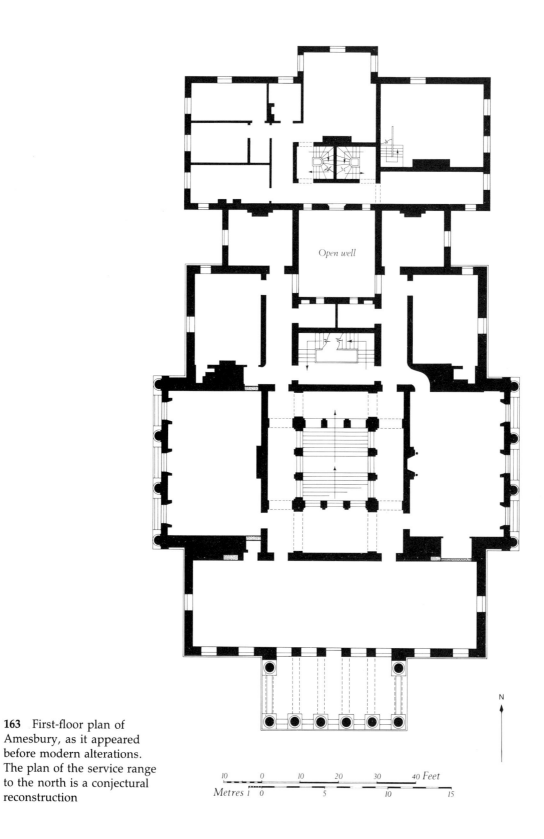

Open well

N

163 First-floor plan of Amesbury, as it appeared before modern alterations. The plan of the service range to the north is a conjectural reconstruction

10   0   10   20   30   40 *Feet*

Metres 1   0   5   10   15

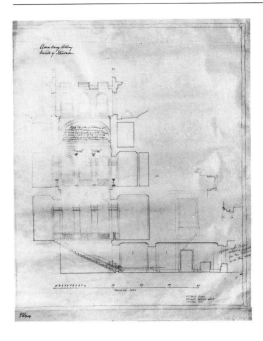

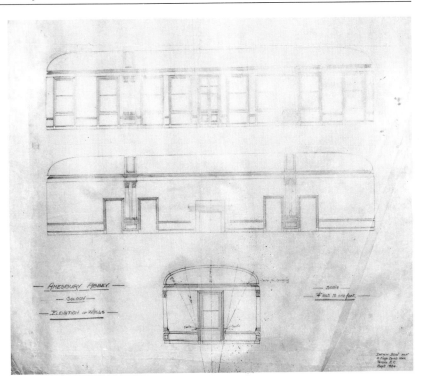

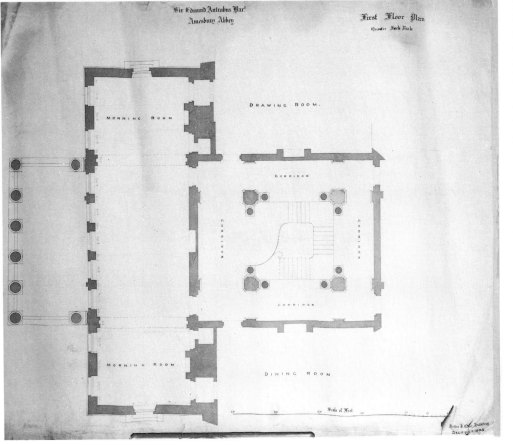

164 (above left) Detmar Blow's section of the stairwell, drawn in 1904, which shows his alterations to the staircase. (RIBA Drawings Collection)

165 (above right) Detmar Blow's drawing for the refitting of the saloon, 1904. (RIBA Drawings Collection)

166 (left) J J Cole's first-floor plan of 1885, showing Hopper's original staircase. (RIBA Drawings Collection)

167 Diana's House, from the south

168 Diana's House, from the south-east

169 Kent House, from the east

Related Structures

Diana's House and Kent House

These two gazebos to the east of the Abbey are dated respectively 1600 and 1607 [**167–9**]. Originally intended as adjuncts to the Abbey, possibly for only occasional use, they are now permanently occupied. Both are of flint with ashlar dressings, of two storeys, pentagonal in plan, with adjoining hexagonal stair towers which rise a storey higher to act as belvederes [**170**]. There is just one room on each floor, the upper being in both cases the more important, having a higher ceiling. As both buildings have original chimneys, they clearly were intended for both winter and summer use. The inscription 'Diana her hous 1600' over the entrance door of the earlier building [**171**] suggests that this was possibly used as a hunting lodge.[73] Kent House might have gained its name from a former lodge occupied by Peter Kent, 'collector of rents' for the Earl of Hertford in 1544.[74] It is dated on a square panel on the stair turret. In the later eighteenth century, Kent House was extended by a large hexagonal room and entrance hall, both with cellars below and a second floor above. The additions are of high quality, and it has been suggested that as tradition ascribes their commissioning to the Duchess of Queensberry, their design might have been by Flitcroft, who received a payment of £300 from her in 1761 for unspecified works.[75]

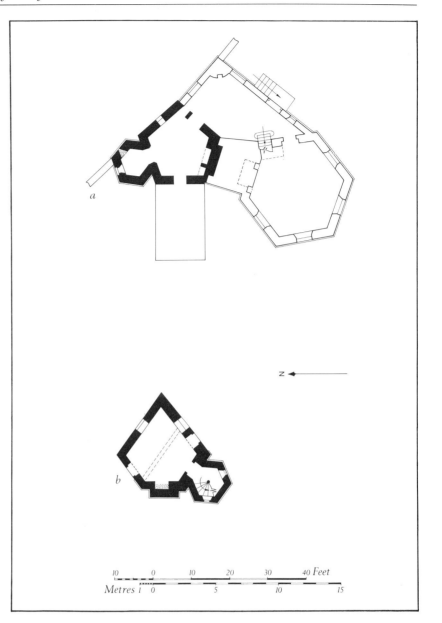

170a Kent House, ground plan. The original building is shown in black. The staircase in the original stair turret at this level has been removed, probably at the time of the eighteenth-century additions

170b Diana's House, ground plan

171 Diana's House, entrance door and inscription

Gay's Cave

Gay's Cave, a rectangular, groin-vaulted chamber with an apse beyond, stands on the part of the park which was planted by Bridgeman west of the River Avon. It is shown with its associated walks and planting on his plan of 1738.[76] The land was not acquired until 1734, two years after John Gay's death, so the naming of the grotto appears to have been sentimental in intent.[77] Entry is made into the stone room through a rusticated, pedimented gateway, with wrought-iron gates. The cave's design has been attributed by Miss Juliet Allan to Flitcroft, being well within his idiom, 'its orthodox Palladian lines barely disguised by a typically formal attempt at rusticity'.[78]

Baluster Bridge

This bridge [172], which has been attributed to the civil engineer, John Smeaton,[79] is dated on a platband 'MDCCLXXVII'. The design with its three elliptical arches, vase-shaped balusters, and large, scrolled terminations represents the most ornamental of his schemes for bridges. A bridge is shown clearly in this position on Bridgeman's plan of 1738, and Dr Pococke admired a 'handsome stone bridge over the river' in 1754.[80] The date of 1777 appears to refer therefore to a rebuilding of an existing structure.

Gate-piers on Church Street, and adjacent to Kent House

The original John Webb house appears from the maps by Flitcroft (1726)[81] and Bridgeman (1738)[82] to have been fronted by a circular, walled forecourt. This was still there in 1773[83] but by the time of the Buckler drawing of 1805 it had been removed.[84] It is suggested that the gate-piers [174], which presently give access to the grounds from Church Street, originally formed the entrance to the forecourt and therefore that they were re-sited between 1773 and 1805 at the time of the creation of the south drive. The gates were recorded by Wyatt Papworth in a drawing made in 1841 from measurements taken in 1817 [173].[85]

The piers are of ashlar, of basically rectangular plan, with round-headed niches to front and rear and plain tablets above, flanked by a Tuscan order carrying a pediment. On the north side, the order is of pilasters, but on the south entrance side it is of sheathed half columns of Serlian inspiration.[86] These

172 The Baluster Bridge

·ELEVATION·OF·THE·GATEWAY·

·AT·AMESBURY·HOUSE·WILTS·

173 Wyatt Papworth's plan and elevation of the gateway. (RIBA Drawings Collection)

174 John Webb's gate-piers, re-sited at the end of the drive which leads to the house

175 The Chinese House, photographed in 1977, before its restoration

175 The Chinese House, photographed in 1977, before its restoration

are strongly reminiscent of Inigo Jones's gate-piers at Holland House,[87] and those in the Jonesian style at Wilton which Colen Campbell published.[88] Thus, with reasonable certainty, they can be attributed to John Webb.[89]

The gate-piers near Kent House are datable stylistically to the early eighteenth century, possibly the 1720s.[90] Of ashlar, with bands of rustication, they are surmounted by cornices, above which are square bases and stone balls. The gates themselves are of nineteenth-century date.

Chinese House
The Chinese House [**175–7**] spans a tributary of the River Avon like a bridge. It is of brick, faced with squared flints dressed with stone, and consists of a single coved room with a doorway at each end, and a large oval window in each long wall. It is surrounded by a continuous verandah which breaks forward to form pedimented porches at the doorways. It is an important, elegant and rare example of eighteenth-century chinoiserie garden architecture, which has been attributed to Sir William Chambers on the grounds of his surviving

correspondence of 1772 with the Duchess of Queensberry, in which it is discussed.[91]

The existence of a building in the Chinese style at Amesbury was noted some time before the period of Chambers' involvement. In the 1748 edition of Defoe's *Tour*, it is remarked that: 'On the Bridge, over the River, is built a Room after the Manner of the Chinese'.[92] The Reverend Woodyeare in 1750[93] and Dr Pococke in 1754[94] also noted its existence, and in 1757 Hanway referred to it as: 'an humble imitation of a Chinese house, which is well shaded and agreeable; but it consists only of one room, and is yet unfinished'.[95] The question which is unresolved is whether this building remained unfinished for a further fifteen years, or whether, as recent commentators suggest, it was demolished and replaced by the present structure, possibly because the earlier one was of a merely temporary nature. There is no firm evidence for the latter hypothesis.

It is quite possible, in view of Hanway's remarks, that Chambers was not called in to design a new building for the Duchess at all, but was asked merely for his advice on the decoration of the

176 The Chinese House, after restoration in 1986

existing one. The limited correspondence concerns the 'embellishing & Elegantifiing' of the 'by name Chinese house', a phrase which in itself suggests that the building was not newly established.[96] The Duchess reminded the architect of a hurried conversation in which she had urged that a moulding of 'Oake leaves & Acorns' was to be preferred to 'Eggs & Anchors'. Also, having seen the work which he had done at Longford Castle, the Duchess recommended that Theodore de Bruyn should be approached to paint the interior, although whether he was approached or not is unknown; there is certainly no surviving decoration by him.

It might be questioned whether a building such as Hanway described would have merited the calling-in, several years later, of an architect of the stature of Chambers, but it is apparent from his letter-books that there had already been correspondence with the Duchess earlier in 1772 about the plans of Amesbury which James Paine had made,[97] and he was also regularly in the area in connection with work at Wilton. In these circumstances it is surely very likely that the Duchess, prompted by his

availability, should seek the advice of the author of *Designs of Chinese Buildings* in completing a project begun some twenty-five years earlier, during the heyday of garden buildings in the 'Chinese taste', and left unfinished as more pressing work was begun on Amesbury Abbey itself.

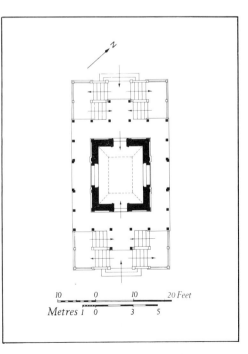

177 The Chinese House, plan

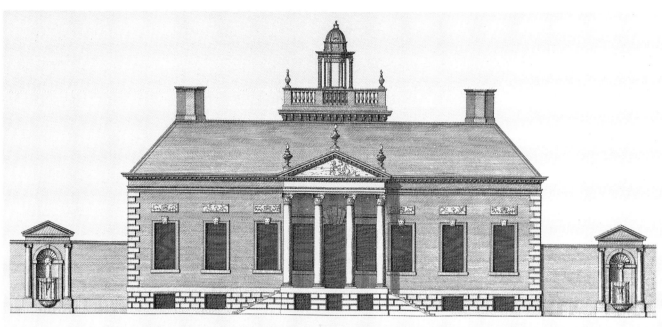

a Scale of 25 Feet.
Extends 82.

The Elevation of Wilberry house in the County of Wilt the Seat of William Benson Esq: Invented and built by himself in the Stile of Inigo Iones. to whom this Plate is most humbly Inscribed.

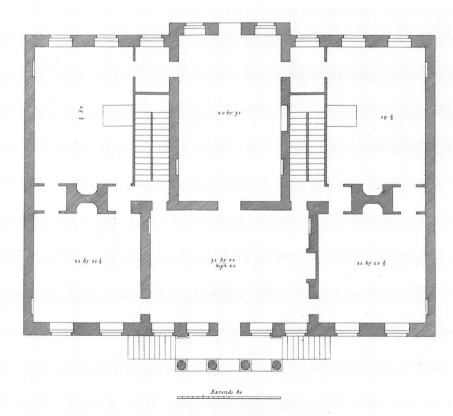

Extends 80

Plan of the principal Floor of Wilberry house.

178 Wilbury, the south front. (Colen Campbell, *Vitruvius Britannicus*, i, 1715)

179 Wilbury, the original ground plan. (Colen Campell, *Vitruvius Britannicus*, i, 1715)

Wilbury House

Ownership and Outline History

Land in the parish of Newton Toney was purchased *c.* 1650 by Colonel Nathaniel Fiennes, father of Celia, the traveller who was born there in 1662.[1] In 1709, an estate in this parish was sold by the family to William Benson, who at that time held a lease of Amesbury Abbey, five miles away.[2] We might follow Christopher Hussey in surmising that Benson, being an ambitious young man of means, was buying land partly in order to give himself the appropriate standing for a political career. In 1710 he served as High Sheriff of Wiltshire and during the same year commenced the building of a new house, Wilbury, a precocious example of the Inigo Jones revival.

Wilbury was designed as a small occasional residence, a villa rather than a country seat.[3] As such it provided the ideal base for Benson's nephew, Henry Hoare the Younger, of the banking family, who bought it from his uncle in 1734 for £14,000. This was some years after inheriting the unfinished Stourhead, which, however, remained the home of his mother, the former Jane Benson during her lifetime.[4] Following her death in 1741, Henry Hoare came into full occupation of Stourhead and sold Wilbury to Fulke Greville, the only

son of Algernon, the second son of Fulke, 5th Baron Brooke. Both Hoare and Greville were responsible for decorative embellishments to the interior of Wilbury, but since Andrews' and Dury's map of 1773[5] shows the Benson cupola to be still *in situ*, the adding of a full second storey to the original single storey and attics must have taken place either towards the end of Greville's ownership, or during that of Thomas Bradshaw who is said to have bought the house in about 1780.[6] He in turn sold it in 1803[7] to Sir Charles Warre Malet, in whose family it remained until its sale in *c.* 1926 to Major Despencer-Robertson MP. In 1939 the estate passed to a new purchaser, Edward Charles Grenfell, 1st Baron St Just; the house remains in the ownership of the family.[8]

The House of 1710

A plan and elevation of Wilbury were published by Colen Campbell in the first volume of *Vitruvius Britannicus* [178, 179] where he described it as the seat of William Benson 'invented and built by himself in the style of Inigo Jones'.[9] With one remarkable bound, Benson had placed himself in the vanguard of architectural taste, and the idea has been floated therefore that he might have had

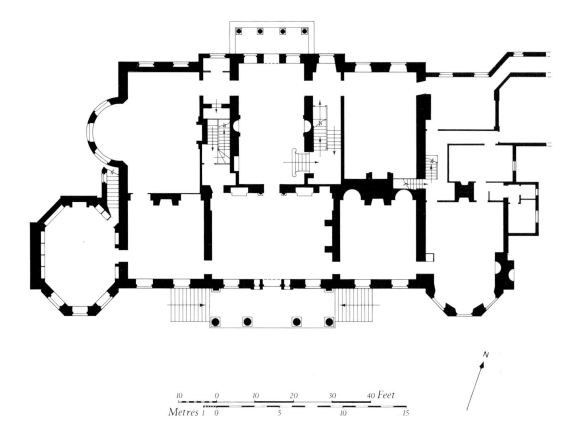

N

180 Ground plan

professional assistance, possibly from Campbell himself, although he also at this date was scarcely embarked upon his architectural career and, on the evidence of his designing Shawfield in 1711, was still in Scotland when Benson began.[10]

Benson did not start entirely from scratch. In 1932, Avray Tipping reported that Major Despencer-Robertson had 'found during the course of alterations interior walls composed of oak framing, with places for doors and windows, quite incompatible as to levels and character with anything William Benson built'.[11] Tipping tended to the view that if an older structure was incorporated in the Benson house, it was likely to have been no more than a hunting lodge. It seems quite reasonable that there should have been some sort of dwelling on an estate like this, and equally reasonable that Benson would have been reticent about starting completely afresh. His model for his new house was Webb's Amesbury,

with which as tenant he was obviously closely familiar. Wilbury covers the same ground area as Amesbury, but Webb's building is here reduced to a single, porticoed main storey with basement and attics. In effect, Webb's main floor has been brought down and placed upon a low, rusticated basement.

The plan also is inspired by that of Amesbury, but a crucial difference of requirement made it more Palladian than its model: a grand staircase was not needed with such limited accommodation on other floors. Benson laid out the centre of his house with the typically Palladian T-shaped conformation of entrance hall and saloon, filling the angles of the T with two identical, modest staircases [**180**], an arrangement for which he was indebted to Palladio's published design for the Villa Poiana [**182**].[12] Also Palladian was the material used by Benson: rendered brick with stone dressings on a stone basement.

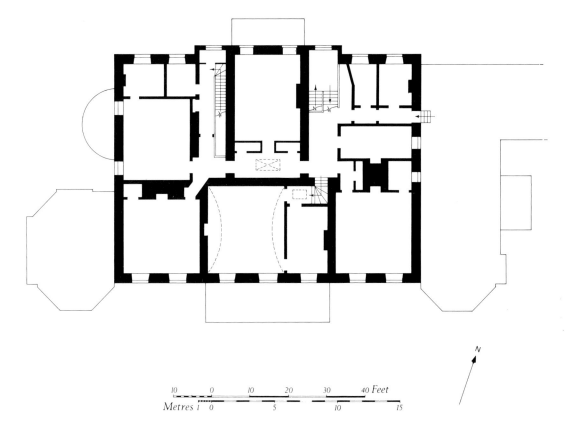

181 First-floor plan

The original flanking walls illustrated by Campbell contained niches set within pedimented aedicules which were intended perhaps as a further reference to Amesbury, this time to Webb's gate-piers.

Benson's original ground plan largely survives. The coved ceiling of the 22' high garden hall limited the upstairs accommodation to attic rooms which appear to have been lit only by windows on the north side of the house. Campbell's elevation of the south front shows decorative stone tablets carved with swags, in place of upper windows. A recently discovered drawing of the house, made during the period of Fulke Greville's ownership, confirms the existence of these panels and indeed the general accuracy of Campbell's rendering. But, as might be expected, it suggests that certain details and proportions were improved for publication purposes, most notably the

inclusion by Campbell of quoins which do not appear on the later drawing.[13] The kitchen and service rooms were placed in the basement with original external access on the east side beneath the present dining-room. Access between the main floor and the basement and attic was by the two staircases, identical on plan, which appear to have risen the full height of the house [**181**]. One of these original stairs survives, situated to the west of the entrance hall [**183**], although its gallimaufry of turned balusters suggests that it has had some alterations. The other, to the east, was replaced in the later eighteenth century by a rather grander main staircase which rose from the ground, rather than from the basement, to the upper floor. It has balusters of octagonal shape and columnar mahogany newels.

Although entrance to the house is now from the north [**184**], the published plan suggests entry through the south front

182 A Palladio, the Villa
Poiana. (*I Quattro Libri
dell'Architettura*, II, 1570)

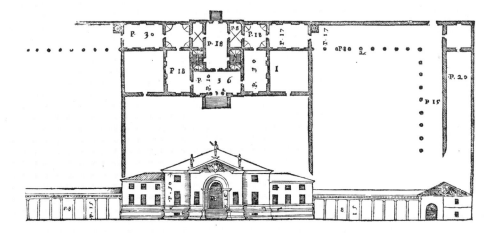

portico directly into the two-storey
garden hall [**185**], from which there is
easy access to the staircases and all
rooms. The removal of the main entrance
from south to north has posed considerable problems of circulation. With the
change in orientation, the route from
entrance to stairs became inconveniently
tortuous, involving passage through the
house into the garden hall. The lobbies
to either side of the north entrance were
partitioned off from the stairs and gave
access only to the bedrooms (identified
by their beds on Campbell's plan). This

arrangement was changed later by the
removal of the partition wall in the east
lobby and the insertion of a door in the
western one. The western lobby now has
rococo decoration [**186**] which suggests
that the alteration might have taken place
in the 1740s or 1750s.

A door was also cut through at the
southern end of the east wall of the hall
to permit direct access to the main stair.
At the same time the door in the garden
hall which gave on to the stair was
blocked.

As published, Benson's plan for the
side ranges of the house, with chimney-
stacks flanked by lobbies and closets,
which divided the rooms and provided
for access between them, directly
followed Webb's arrangement. The chimney-stack and adjacent lobby and closet
in the west bedroom (later the ballroom)
was removed in the early nineteenth
century when a new fireplace was
inserted in its east wall. The presence of
Jonesian round-headed openings in the
north wall of the present drawing-room
(the original parlour), one of which is
now blocked, suggests that this arrangement was executed as shown on the
Campbell plan. The subsequent closure
of an opening, and the removal of the
original door from the west bedroom to
the stair, has considerably hampered
circulation in this part of the house.

On the eastern side there must be

183 Original staircase to the
west of the hall

184 The north, present entrance hall

185 The south, garden hall, formerly the entrance hall

186 Ceiling of the lobby to the west of the north hall

187 Composite capital in the garden hall

page 131

189 Chimney-piece and overmantel in the garden hall

188 The original dining-room to the east of the garden hall

considerable doubt as to whether the arrangement of spaces on the published plan was followed at all. The door openings to lobby and closet shown by Campbell in the north wall of the original dining-room (the present boudoir) are occupied by round-headed alcoves which appear to be original. If they are, then access from the dining-room to the bedroom must have involved going through the garden hall. However, there remains the possibility that these alcoves represent the later blocking of doors, in a style in keeping with the original decoration. Taken in conjunction with the blocking of the door in the north-east corner of the garden hall, this has resulted in access from the original dining-room [188] to the adjacent bedroom (the present dining-room) involving passage not only through the garden hall but through the entrance hall also.

The garden hall in Benson's house is thus the architectural focus, not only for reasons of grandeur but also for reasons of convenience. It was and remains an integral part of the circulatory space. As a piece of planning the arrangement can never have been satisfactory, and the efficacy of Webb's corridor arrangement at Amesbury is appreciated all the more, by reason of its absence here.

In terms of decorative achievement, the garden hall is the most impressive room in the house. Some of Benson's detailing survives. The chimney-piece with reeded pilasters and heavy volutes [189] is original, but its elegant architrave of scrolls and foliage, referred to by Hussey and shown in a photograph of 1932, has gone, to be replaced by rather effete palm fronds.[14] The raised octagons in the coving of the ceiling, simulating coffering, probably represent an attempt at the antique *gravitas* which was considered appropriate in a neo-Palladian house. Also by Benson (the idea taken directly from the Amesbury saloon) is the central door with broken pediment and composite capitals [187], incorporating unicorns' heads (bearded, with vestigial horns) which are without any apparent emblematic significance. The wall frames with eared corners, and the bas-relief of boys and a dolphin above the chimney-piece, were probably decorative additions made by Hoare, whilst the style of the frieze of flowers and masks, the medallions framing busts and the stucco drops illustrative of music, the theatre, hunting and gardening, indicate a still later rococo decorative phase, perhaps of the 1740s or 1750s. The unusual scagliola floor might also be of this date.

There are no original fittings surviving on the first floor but in the attic room over the garden hall there is a re-sited early eighteenth-century bolection-moulded chimney-piece. Another chimney-piece of the same period survives in the basement beneath the ballroom.

The House in the later Eighteenth Century

The problem of the limited accommodation afforded by the original house was solved in the later eighteenth century by increasing the attic to full storey height (involving the loss of the cupola) and by the addition of low wings with canted south bays [190]. The southern aspect of the house, after these alterations, is recorded in a view published in 1813

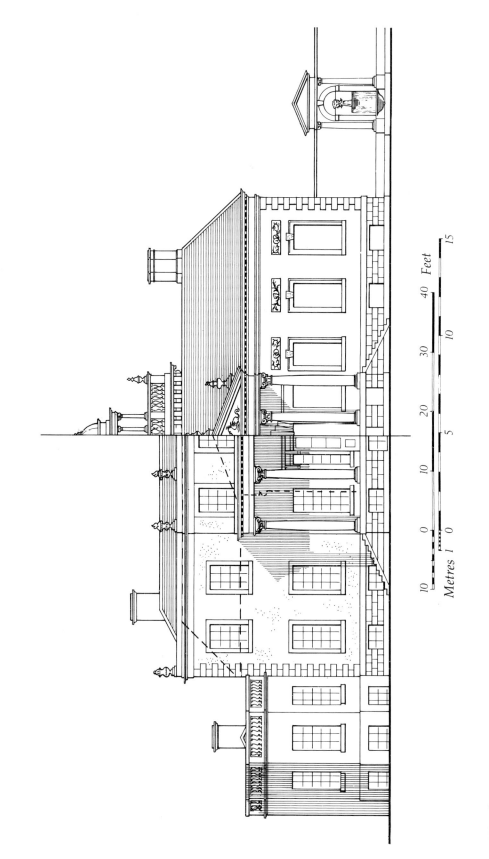

Metres 1   0

Feet

190   Comparative drawing of the original and extended houses

[**191**].[15] This shows that the original nine windows of the main floor were reduced to seven, and that the portico had been rebuilt to extend the full width of the garden hall, an extension which, together with a deep pediment, gave it a rustically squat appearance reminiscent of Inigo Jones's St Paul's, Covent Garden. On the north front, the original shallow projection of the entrance hall was extended by two bays to bring it to the same width as the south front portico.

The flanking wing to the west comprises an octagonal library with elegant neo-classical fittings; that to the east has a bedroom which was originally built as a Roman Catholic chapel, registered by Thomas Bradshaw and his chaplain, Abbé Benoist, in 1797[16] and identified as such now by a late nineteenth-century semicircular panel in the ceiling coving displaying a winged cherub at the apex of a sea of radiating feathers.[17] To the north, the present kitchen was probably built as a priest's room. The wings took the place of the flanking walls illustrated in both Campbell's engraving and the later Greville period drawing.

The ballroom, formerly the drawing-room and originally a bedroom, is the fashionable creation of the early nineteenth century. Its construction involved the removal of the lobby, closet and chimney-stack to the south, and the insertion of a fireplace in the east wall. This has a white marble surround of the period. Further space was gained by the addition of a large projecting semicircular bow to the west [**193**]. This improvement was part of the final stage of alterations to the house which occurred after its purchase by Sir Charles Malet in 1803, Britton reporting in 1825 that 'great improvements have been made in the property since that time'.[18] Malet's other alterations involved the addition of an ionic portico to the entrance front [**196**], and after 1813, the date of the engraved view from the south, the heightening of the south portico. This involved the removal of its pediment and the installing above of a row of three windows, positioned higher than those to either side, to light the newly created attic rooms above the garden hall [**192**].

Wilbury by this time had grown beyond being the villa designed for occasional use, as conceived by Benson, and had become, in the opinion of Britton, 'a handsome edifice, adapted for the comfortable accommodation of a family'.[19]

Related Structures

The octagonal, domed summerhouse [**194**] north of the house is of early to mid eighteenth-century date. Of rendered brick on an ashlar plinth, it is articulated by Tuscan half-columns with banded rustication. A stone records a restoration carried out in 1899 by 'ACWM'.

The summerhouse sits on a low mound over a circular grotto [**197**], about 11' wide, with a domed vault of flint and stone. It is entered from the east by a segmental arched tunnel. The adjacent arch noted by Pevsner[20] has been demolished.

North of the house, two urns on pedestals, commemorating Admirals Nelson and Cornwallis, flank the entry to an avenue, at the end of which is a fluted doric column with an urn finial, dedicated to Queen Victoria and dated 1877.

To the west of the house, a grotto of Greek cross plan is buried in a bank. It is of flint with brick dressings, its four apses framed by pointed brick arches.[21]

On the south side of the house, a carved fragment, being half a four-centred stone doorhead, is inscribed '. . . HIS TOWER 1600' [**195**]. The resemblance is so close to the doorhead inscribed 'DIANA HER HOUS 1600' at Amesbury that it might be presumed that Benson removed it from Amesbury with the intention of re-using it, perhaps in the now vanished tower known as 'Benson's Folly'.[22]

To the east is a range of stables, of late eighteenth and nineteenth-century date, built of brick and flint in banded courses.

191 Wilbury from the south, after alterations, in an engraving published in 1813

192 (below) The south front

page 135

193 (above left) The bow added to the west side in the early nineteenth century

194 (centre) The circular grotto beneath the summerhouse

195 Inscribed doorhead; *see also* **171**

196 (above right) The north front and forecourt

197 (below right) The summerhouse

The East front of Stourhead in Wiltshire the Seat of Henry Hoare Esq.

198 The east front. The projecting portico was not built until 1841. (Colen Campbell, *Vitruvius Britannicus*, III, 1725)

199 Plans of the ground floor 'as design'd by Mr Campbell' and 'as executed by Mr Hoare'. (Colen Campbell, *Vitruvius Britannicus*, III, 1725) Hoare's most notable alteration, in the interests of convenience and privacy, was to substitute a centrally placed service stair for the two spiral stairs proposed by Campbell

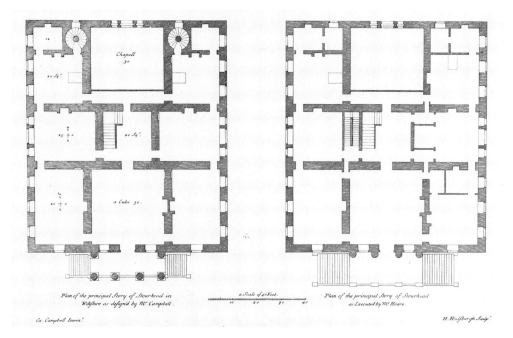

Plan of the principal Story of Stourhead in Wiltshire as design'd by Mr Campbell.

a Scale of 40 Feet

Plan of the principal Story of Stourhead as Executed by Mr Hoare.

Related Wiltshire Palladian Buildings

Stourhead

The work of Colen Campbell was of crucial importance in the establishment and dissemination of English neo-Palladianism as a national style, for in addition to his role as an adept publicist, he produced designs of great typological significance: the Palladian great house at Wanstead, Essex; the rotunda at Mere-worth, Kent; and the villas at Newby, Yorkshire, and Stourhead, Wiltshire.

Work on the demolition of the old house at Stourton was begun in 1719 for Henry Hoare, who commissioned Campbell's designs for a new house [198–200]. These were published in 1725, the year of Hoare's death. Henry Hoare the Younger did not come into the property, which had become 'Stourhead' in 1723, until after the death of his mother in 1741, but it is likely that he was actively engaged in the fitting up of the house, which continued for some years after its completion in 1724.[1]

Campbell derived his design from Palladio's published plan and elevation of the Villa Emo at Fanzolo [201].[2] The house was rather larger than its five-bay frontage would suggest, being deeper than it was wide. The portico *in antis* of the Villa Emo became in Campbell's design a projecting portico, although the design was changed during the building campaign and an applied portico was constructed [202]. The projecting portico was built eventually in 1841.

The main rooms were situated in the Palladian manner at *piano nobile* level, over the rusticated basement service area. Entry was made via steps directly into the entrance hall, a cube room of 30', with the grand, centrally placed staircase beyond, and at the rear of the house, a chapel, flanked by bedchambers with connecting dressing-rooms. Drawing and dining-rooms were placed to either side of the stairs, and the Music Room and Cabinet Room to either side of the hall.

Whilst the entrance front of Stourhead [203] was derived from Palladio, the side elevations combined ideas which Campbell was developing for Houghton with clear reminiscences of the south front of Wilton.

Stourhead does not survive intact. Wings were added by Sir Richard Colt Hoare, the antiquary, in 1793–5, to house a picture gallery and library and, following a fire in 1902 which gutted the centre of the house, it was reconstructed with some alterations.[3]

Stourhead is close to Amesbury and it was probably there that Henry Hoare met Flitcroft. He employed the architect

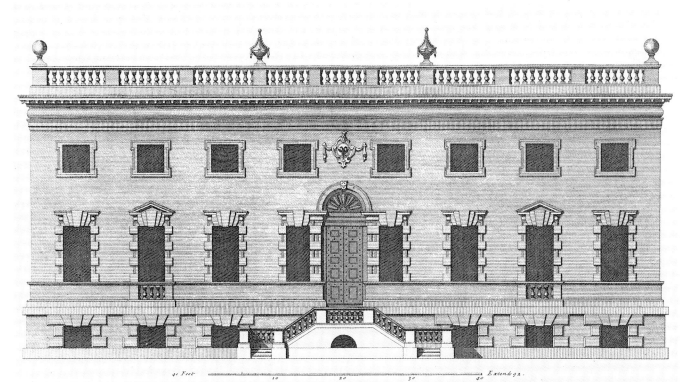

The Garden or South front of Stourhead in Wiltshire

200   The south, garden front. (Colen Campbell, *Vitruvius Britannicus*, III, 1725); *see also* **11**

201   A Palladio, the Villa Emo. (*I Quattro Libri dell'Architettura*, II, 1570)

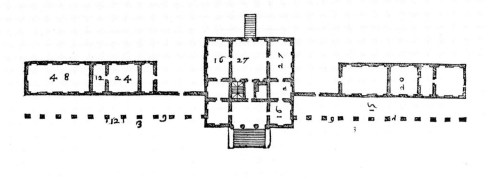

202 Stourhead from the east, published by J Neale, 1822. (*Views of the Seats of Noblemen and Gentlemen*, v)

203 The east front

from 1744 on the designing of buildings which still adorn the justly celebrated landscaped grounds of his house. As the Wilton grounds and water-works are pre-eminent in the history of the early seventeenth-century formal garden, so is Stourhead (together with Stowe) the pre-eminent example of the contrivedly natural, picturesque, Claudian landscape, which formed the ideal setting for the formal Palladian house and its carefully sited garden buildings.[4]

Flitcroft was responsible for the Temple of Ceres (1744–5), later known as the Temple of Flora [204], a single room with a projecting Doric portico; the Pantheon (1754–6) [205], a domed rotunda with a Corinthian portico *in antis*; the Temple of Apollo (1765) [206], a rotunda with detached Corinthian columns and a scalloped entablature, based on the Round Temple at Baalbec, which had been published in 1757;[5] and a structure with very different historical associations, Alfred's Tower, a 160' high triangular tower with round angle projections, designed *c*. 1765 but not completed until 1772, after the architect's death. It is said to commemorate the place where King Alfred rallied his forces before repelling the invading Danes in AD 878.

Tottenham Park

The history of Tottenham Park [207–9] has been established in recent years and it serves no useful purpose to rehearse the whole story here, but the importance of the house in the context of neo-Palladianism is such that a summary is desirable.[1]

Tottenham, situated in Savernake Forest, was owned by the Bruce family who in the later years of the seventeenth century were also the owners of Amesbury. Charles, Lord Bruce, invited his brother-in-law, Lord Burlington, to design and build him a new house *c*. 1720 to replace the old family seat which recently had been destroyed by fire. Flitcroft was Burlington's executant architect for the work.

Burlington's first proposals incorporated Palladian towers in the manner of Palladio's Villa Pisani[2] (and Wilton), and the basilical, columned hall and imperial staircase of Webb's Gunnersbury. As the design evolved in the early 1720s, further influences came into play. The central tower of Webb's Amesbury[3] was introduced to light an alternative grand central stair, the flanking towers on the entrance side acquired Venetian windows, and a flat-topped portico adapted from the south front loggia of Inigo Jones's Queen's House was added to the garden side. Later, towers were added to the garden side as well to make Tottenham a four-towered house. In the meantime, the plan, with reference to the Villas Pisani and Sarego [210,211],[4] evolved in a Palladian rather than an Anglo-Palladian manner, with the grand central stairs and tower abandoned in favour of two identical, separate, narrow flights to either side of the central hall.

The four towers of Tottenham gave the house the appearance of a smaller version of Holkham, the design of which Lord Burlington was working upon with William Kent in the 1730s. The wings which Burlington added to Tottenham from *c.* 1730 underline this similarity, for they were in the staccato manner in their separation of elements [212], each of the pavilions being made up of three separately roofed units.

Tottenham was found to be lacking in accommodation and deficient in services in the nineteenth century, and Thomas Cundy was employed from *c.* 1825 to put matters right. The rebuilder, Charles

208 Elevation of the garden front, after the addition of the towers, drawn by Henry Flitcroft. (Devonshire Collection, Chatsworth)

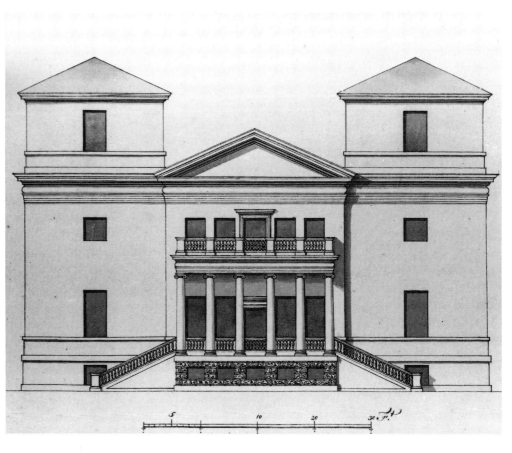

209 Plan of the ground floor, showing the house after the addition of the wings. (Devonshire Collection, Chatsworth)

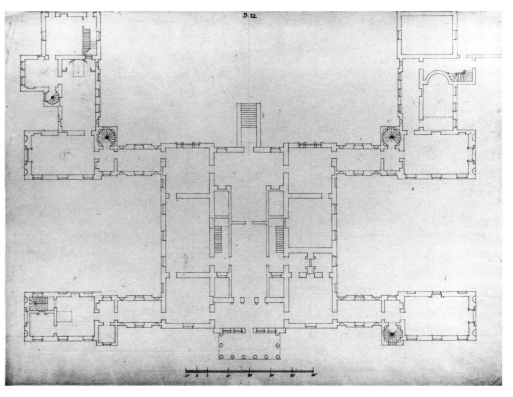

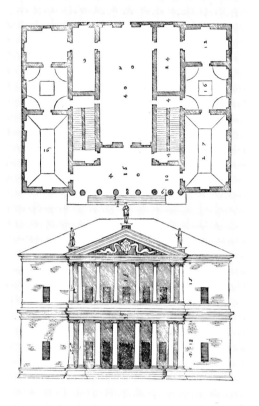

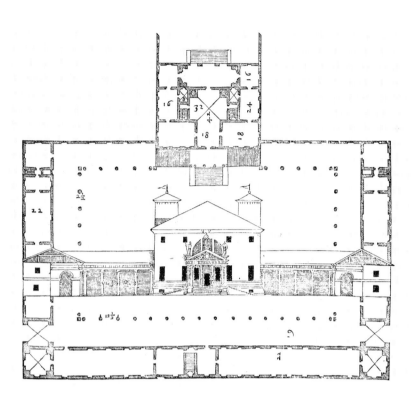

210 A Palladio, the Villa Pisani. (*I Quattro Libri dell'Architettura*, ıı, 1570)

211 A Palladio, the Villa Sarego. (*I Quattro Libri dell'Architettura*, ıı, 1570)

212 (left) Tottenham Park, the garden front, published by J Neale, 1822. (*Views of the Seats of Noblemen and Gentlemen*, v)

213 Thomas Cundy's
rebuilt Tottenham Park

Brudenell-Bruce, Marquess of Ailesbury, was advised by his cousin, Sir Richard Colt Hoare of Stourhead, to 'Look before you leap and see if you cannot make your house comfortable without going to so great an expense'. But, in the words of the Earl of Cardigan, 'Charles, Marquess of Ailesbury . . . was not given to looking before he leaped'. Burlington's house was swallowed up by Cundy's extensive enlargements and sumptuous remodelling [213], only one of the rooms retaining its original Palladian details.[5]

In the grounds of Tottenham there is an octagonal summer-house, designed and built by Burlington in 1743. He also designed the banqueting house in the woods which was demolished in 1824.[6]

Lydiard Park

John, 2nd Viscount St John, succeeded to his father's title in 1742 and commenced the remodelling of the family's country seat at Lydiard Tregoze in the following year. The existing house was of traditional form: a central hall with projecting cross wings. It probably dated from the sixteenth century but a survey drawing on a map of *c*. 1700 [214] suggests that the house was refaced, perhaps in the later seventeenth century.[1]

Viscount St John's intention in the works begun in 1743 was to remodel the house to provide two symmetrical classical façades at right angles to each other, fronting a new suite of state rooms, with a grand entrance in one of the fronts into a newly constructed hall which replaced the original recessed entrance. He hoped perhaps that visitors seeing the house from across the park would presume that the house was quadrangular, its two show fronts implying the presence of further ranges behind.

The identity of St John's architect is not documented but the house has been attributed to Roger Morris.[2] Certainly the architect of the remodelled Lydiard was a Palladian designer of quality, and some similarities with Wilton would suggest the presence of an architect familiar with that house, as Morris was.

The imposition of a strictly formal exterior [216] on a less than regular plan [215] has led to eccentricities and irregularities in the arrangement of rooms and the spacing of windows. The corner towers, inspired by Wilton but with pyramidal roofs are, like their model, set on the same plane as the façade with quoins laid upon the surface to articulate the wall rather than to define an angle. It might be that these towers are afterthoughts, although the articulation of the plinth base, prepared to receive them, would suggest otherwise. It is more likely that, as at Wilton, the lines of the façade were determined by the original foundations of the house and it would have been too expensive to attempt a more radical rebuilding.

Inside, there is some evidence to suggest that the design was modified during building. A flat and comparatively low ceiling was intended for the hall, but a higher, coved ceiling was constructed which cuts across the first-floor windows of the entrance front and blocks the doors which were placed at first-floor level to provide access into the room over the hall. Because of the exigencies of the existing plan, the hall could not be a cube room, but by raising the ceiling the architect was able to make the dimensions approximate more closely to the neo-Palladian ideal.

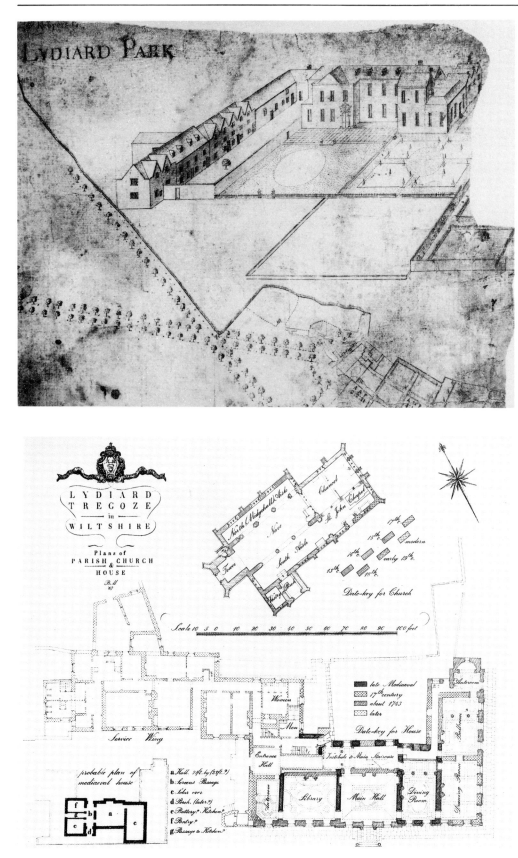

214 Survey drawing of *c*. 1700. (Warwickshire Record Office, CR 162/714, Ward-Boughton-Leigh Archives)

215 Plan of Lydiard Park showing development phases

216 Lydiard Park, the
eighteenth-century front
(*Country Life*)

Postscript

Fischer von Erlach, the great architect of the Austrian baroque, predicated his vast, comparative history of architecture, the *Entwurff Einer Historischen Architectur*, published in 1721, on the idea of the unbroken, historical progression. A continuous line, albeit wavering, could be traced from the Temple of Solomon to the work of his own day. At much the same time, in advancing the case of Palladio and of Inigo Jones, the British Vitruvius, Colen Campbell was asserting a comparable historical continuity. The brief moment of English neo-Palladianism provides us with the tangible evidence of this optimistic view of the world and man's place in it.

Throughout the seventeenth century, philosophers had engaged with the great issues of religious and scientific truth, Bacon keeping them separate in an uneasy dualism, Hobbes postulating a corporeal universe but admitting the possibility of a Day of Judgement resurrection, and Locke arguing for the absorption of the one by the other in a view of nature as a rational system of divine laws. The 3rd Earl of Shaftesbury consolidated this position by propounding a view of nature as a system of interconnected and interdependent parts, divinely perfect. To see how far philosophy had travelled in a short space of time to reach this position, we need look no further than Shaftesbury's own grandfather, the 1st Earl, Dryden's Achitophel, who is said to have dabbled in such arcana as alchemy, palmistry and the casting of horoscopes.

Neo-Palladianism, for the early eighteenth-century Englishman, provided a rational architectural style for this rational and divinely perfect age. The authority of antiquity in providing a model was unquestionable and Palladio was the medium through whom that rational interpretation was transmitted.

Such moments of equilibrium as this are rare. The spirit of rapturous contemplation which informed Shaftesbury's vision could not last and the emphasis of the philosophers of the eighteenth century shifted, critically, towards the sensibilities. David Hume upset the certainties and revealed the limitations of reason by finding it to be nothing more than a member of the species of sensations. Edmund Burke went further, finding in man a mass of predispositions inherited from an incalculable past, with no absolutes possible. In an age in which the inevitable progression of history could be so dramatically thrown open to question, the unbroken line could no longer be accepted. Antiquity was no longer sacrosanct; the ancients could be not only equalled but surpassed, and a new age of architectural experimentation dawned, informed by a more sophisticated view of the past which paradoxically prompted an investigation of origins which was at once more romantic and more archaeological.

The Wiltshire houses which we have been considering reflect the broader philosophical developments of the seventeenth and earlier eighteenth centuries. From the elegant, flawed compromise of Wilton, through the vigorous experimentation of Amesbury, we arrive via the inchoate Wilbury at the silent stasis of Stourhead and Tottenham. Lydiard Park is merely a coda prior to the onset of disintegration.

Notes

The National Context

1 K Downes 1984. The Publication of Shaftesbury's *Letter Concerning Design*. *Architectural History* **27**, pp 519–23

2 Anthony, Earl of Shaftesbury 1732. *Characteristicks of Men, Manners, Opinions, Times*, III, 5th edn, pp 395–410

3 C Campbell 1715. For the genesis of *Vitruvius Britannicus* and Campbell's role, *see* E Harris 1986. *Vitruvius Britannicus* before Colen Campbell, *Burlington Magazine* **CXXVIII**, pp 340–6

4 Quoted by J Webb 1665. *A Vindication of Stone-Heng Restored*, p 182. Reprinted by Gregg International Publishers, 1971

5 H M Colvin 1978, p 870

6 H M Colvin and J Newman 1981, p 23

7 R Wittkower 1974, pp 76–8

8 Ibid pp 79–81. Wittkower's suggestion that Leoni's first book appeared in 1716 rather than in 1715 is contradicted by T Connor in 1977 in The Making of *Vitruvius Britannicus*. *Architectural History* **20** pp 20, 28
Both Leoni and Pellegrini worked at Schloss Bensberg. It is suggested that Leoni's departure for London from the Palatinate followed Pellegrini's arrival at the Court of the Elector, but the known dates of the various arrivals and departures are such that it is equally arguable that Leoni came to London first and advised Pellegrini to go to Bensberg.

9 G Knox 1985. Sebastiano Ricci at Burlington House: a Venetian decoration *alla Romana*. *Burlington Magazine* **CXXVII**, pp 601–9

10 R Hewlings 1985. James Leoni. In *The Architectural Outsiders*, ed R Brown, Waterstone

11 For Burlington on the Grand Tour, *see* J Lees-Milne 1962, pp 103–22

12 For Burlington's role in sponsoring publications, *see* T Connor. Burlingtonian Publications. In *Lord Burlington and his Circle*, papers given at a Georgian Group symposium, 1982 pp 52–9

13 H M Colvin 1978, p 129

14 *See also* T Hudson 1974. *The Origins of Palladianism in English Eighteenth-Century Architecture*. PhD thesis, University of Cambridge

15 D Cruickshank. An English Reason. *Architectural Review*, April 1983, p 51

16 D Howard and M Longair. Harmonic Proportion and Palladio's *Quattro Libri*. *Journal of the Society of Architectural Historians* **XLI**, 2, May 1982, pp 116–43

17 D Howard. Four Centuries of Literature on Palladio, *Journal of the Society of Architectural Historians* **XXXIX**, 3, October 1980 pp 224–41

18 D Cruickshank 1985, p 51

19 For the Office of Works during this period, *see* H M Colvin 1976. *See also* H M Colvin. Lord Burlington and the Office of Works. In *Lord Burlington and his Circle*, papers given at a Georgian Group symposium, 1982 pp 97–101

20 H M Colvin 1978, pp 108–9

21 H M Colvin. Lord Burlington and the Office of Works. In *Lord Burlington and his Circle*, papers given at a Georgian Group symposium, 1982, p 101

22 R Venturi 1966. *Complexity and Contradiction in Architecture*, Museum of Modern Art, New York, p 25

Wiltshire Palladianism

1 D Defoe 1724–6. *A Tour thro' the Whole Island of Great Britain*, J M Dent & Sons, 1974, p 168

2 C Middleton 1793. *Picturesque and Architectural Views for Cottages, Farm Houses and Country Villas.* Quoted in J Summerson 1959. *Journal of the Royal Society of Arts,* July 1959, p 571

3 In the informed opinion of the Duchess of Queensberry, writing to William Pitt from her seat at Amesbury in 1741, Wilton was 'the finest place in this County' and she hoped that the Prince of Wales would not fail to see it: 'certainly I can take care to clear the coast'. V Biddulph 1935. *Kitty, Duchess of Queensberry.* Nicholson & Watson, p 165

4 The Holkham towers have pyramidal roofs. Those designed by Campbell for Houghton had pedimented gables, but as executed the towers have domes designed by James Gibbs

5 For Brympton d'Evercy *see Country Life* **LXI**, 1927, pp 718–26, 762–9; and N Pevsner 1958. *The Buildings of England: South and West Somerset,* Penguin Books, pp 107–9. For Hinton House *see* N Pevsner 1958. *The Buildings of England: South and West Somerset,* Penguin Books, p 198. For Ashton Court *see* N Pevsner 1958. *The Buildings of England: North Somerset and Bristol,* Penguin Books, pp 220–2

6 J Newman and N Pevsner 1972. *The Buildings of England: Dorset,* Penguin Books, 1972 p 396: H M Colvin 1978, p 256; J Hutchins 1868. *The History and Antiquities of the County of Dorset,* III, reproduces the engraving of the house

7 RCHME 1970. *An Inventory of the Historical Monuments in Dorset* **II**, *South-East,* Part 2, HMSO, p 238

8 RCHME 1975. *An Inventory of the Historical Monuments in Dorset* **V**, *East,* HMSO, pp 7–12

9 Ibid pp 94–7

10 The St Giles's chimney-piece was published as a piece by Jones, along with four Wilton chimney-pieces: J Vardy 1744. *Some Designs of Mr Inigo Jones and Mr Wm. Kent,* p 16

11 J Lees-Milne 1962, p 63

12 For Quarley, *see* K Woodbridge 1970, p 20. With thanks to Ms Clare Clubb, Guildhall Library, London, for information on the ownership of Quarley

13 K Woodbridge 1970, p 26

14 J Lees-Milne 1962, pp 67–71

15 He was so described by Jonathan Richardson the younger; quoted by Brinsley Ford 1985. In Sir Andrew Fountaine – One of the Keenest Virtuosi of his Age, *Apollo* **CXXII**, November 1985, p 363. For Sir Andrew Fountaine, *see also* A W Moore 1985. *Norfolk and the Grand Tour,* Norfolk Museums Service, pp 27–31, 93–113; H M Colvin 1978, pp 319–20

16 *The Norfolk Tour,* 5th edn, 1795, lists the paintings at Narford. Following the list of paintings by Pellegrini, the compiler notes: 'Over the chimney a portrait of Lord Burlington, who made Sir Andrew Fountaine a present of these pictures'. *See also* G Knox, 'Antonio Pellegrini and Marco Ricci: from Burlington House to Narford Hall', *Burlington Magazine,* forthcoming

Wilton House

1 VCH 1956. *A History of Wiltshire,* III, Institute of Historical Research, University of London, pp 231–2

2 The Abbey church was rebuilt by Edith, wife of Edward the Confessor, and was consecrated in 1065. In *c.* 1291 there were probably 80 nuns at the Abbey; by 1441 this number had fallen to 44. Following the surrender of the Abbey to the Crown on 25 March 1539, the Abbess and 32 nuns were granted pensions. *See* D Knowles and R N Hadcock 1971. *Medieval Religious Houses,* Longman, p 268

3 VCH 1962. *A History of Wiltshire,* VI, Institute of Historical Research, University of London, p 2

4 *Survey of the Lands of William, 1st Earl of Pembroke (c.* 1565) WRO 2057/S3. Privately printed for the Roxburghe Club, 1909, ed C R Straton

5 J Nicols 1788. *The Progresses, and Public Processions, of Queen Elizabeth,* I, p 19, entries for 1574

6 J Britton 1847, pp 82–4

7 *See* M Girouard 1978. *Life in the English Country House,* Yale University Press, pp 121–2, where Pembroke's loss of the

office of Lord Chamberlain is cited as a factor in the reduction of the building scheme. L Stone's article, On the Grand Scale, *TLS*, 10 November 1978, in reviewing Girouard, ascribes Pembroke's cancellation of the grand scheme to the need to return his daughter-in-law's dowry. For the Earl's estrangement from his wife *see* G C Williamson 1922. *Lady Anne Clifford*, T Wilson & Son, Kendal

8   Four of Webb's drawings for Durham House are inscribed by him, 'not taken'. J Harris and A A Tait 1979, pp 36–7

9   C Campbell 1717, pl 61–2

10 J M Robinson 1979. *The Wyatts*, Oxford University Press, p 75

11 J H Harvey 1969. *William Worcestre Itineraries*, Clarendon Press, p 53: 'The church of the convent of Wilton . . . is about 90 of my steps long and the nave of the church with its two aisles is about 46 of my steps across.'

12 The Journal of Sir Roger Wilbraham, *The Camden Miscellany* **X**, 3rd series, 4, 1902, p 65

13 Information kindly provided by Mr D Sumpster, Architect with the HBMC: reference has also been made to Historic Buildings Grant files

14 Lieutenant Hammond 1635. Description of a Journey *The Camden Miscellany* **XVI**, 1936, pp 66–8

15 WAS, Devizes

16 J Summerson 1970, p 45

17 J Britton 1847, p 83

18 Lieutenant Hammond 1635. Description of a Journey, *The Camden Miscellany* **XVI**, 1936, pp 66–8

19 J Britton 1847, pp 83–4

20 J Webb 1655. *The most notable Antiquity of Great Britain, vulgarly called Stone-Heng*. Webb stated in his introduction to this volume that it had been 'moulded off, and cast into a rude Form, from some few indigested notes of the late judicious Architect, the Vitruvius of his age Inigo Jones'. The circumstances of the investigation are given on page one, as if written by Jones: 'King James, in his progresse, the year one thousand six hundred

and twenty, being at Wilton, and discoursing of this Antiquity, I was sent for by the right Honourable William then Earl of Pembrook, and received there his Majesties commands to produce out of mine own practise in Architecture, and experience in Antiquities abroad, what possibly I could discover concerning this of Stoneheng'. The volume was dedicated by Webb to Philip, 5th Earl of Pembroke

21 H M Colvin 1954, pp 181–90

22 Ibid p 183

23 A A Tait 1964, p 74

24 I de Caus *c.* 1654

25 J Harris and A A Tait 1979, pp 47–8

26 E Mercer 1962, p 13

27 J Harris and A A Tait 1979, pp 36–7

28 *Catalogue of the Drawings Collection of the RIBA: C-F*, Gregg International Publishers, 1972, p 80, fig 56

29 Information kindly provided by Mr J Harris, formerly Curator of the Drawings Collection of the RIBA

30 Chambers' description of Wilton: RIBA Ms CHA 1/13; *see also* J Harris 1970, pp 251–2

31 A Palladio 1570, II

32 V Scamozzi 1615. *L'Idea della Architettura Universale*, Part I, Book III, p 284

33 G Popper and J Reeves 1982, pp 358–61

34 *See also* P Henderson 1985. Life at the Top, *Country Life*, **CLXXVII**, pp 6–9

35 J Britton 1847, p 85

36 Ibid p 84

37 Churchwardens' Accounts, St Edmund and St Thomas, Salisbury

38 H M Colvin 1954, pp 187–8

39 RCHME 1975. *An Inventory of the Historical Monuments in Dorset* **V**, East Dorset, HMSO, pp 7–12

40 J Britton 1847, p 84

41 G Vertue. Notebooks, v, *Walpole Society* **XXVI** p 25,

42 BL Add 33767B, fo 24; *see also* L Magalotti 1821. *Travels of Cosimo III, Grand Duke of Tuscany, through England, during the reign of Charles the Second*

43 Bodleian Library, Gough Maps 33, 19r

44 H M Colvin 1954, p 189

45 J Evelyn. *The Diary of John Evelyn*, ed E S de Beer, Oxford University Press, 1959, entry for 20 July 1654

46 S Pepys. *The Diary of Samuel Pepys*, ix, 1668–9, eds R C Latham and W Matthews, G Bell & Sons, 1976, p 230, entry for 11 June 1668

47 D Defoe 1748. *A Tour thro' the Whole Island of Great Britain*, i, 4th edn, pp 332–6

48 J A Gotch 1921. Some Newly Found Drawings and Letters of John Webb, *Journal of the Royal Institute of British Architects* **XXVIII**, 3rd series, p 574

49 C Campbell 1717, p 3

50 M Whinney and O Millar 1957, pp 41–2; J Summerson, 1970, p 118

51 WRO, 2057 H1/1a

52 H M Colvin 1976, p 472

53 J Harris and A A Tait 1979, no 60

54 Ibid p 26

55 St Paul's Cathedral, Works Accounts 1–15

56 I am indebted to Gordon Higgott for sharing his ideas on the Jones and Webb drawings, and for kindly allowing me to read the relevant parts of his PhD thesis: *The Architectural Drawings of Inigo Jones: attribution, dating and analysis*, University of London, 1987

57 J Harris 1972, figs 128, 131, 155, 156, 160

58 Ashmolean Museum, *Cotelle Album*. Some of the designs were published in J Cotelle *c.* 1640. *Livre de divers ornemens pour plafonds . . .* See also P Thornton 1978. *Seventeenth Century Interior Decoration in England, France and Holland*, Yale University Press, pp 38, 405

59 J Harris 1972, fig 174

60 Ashmolean Museum, *Cotelle Album*, 89A. *See also* P Thornton 1978, *Seventeenth Century Interior Decoration in England, France and Holland*, pp 69, 406

61 WHA, 2057 A5/1; Sidney, 16th Earl of Pembroke 1968, p 89; E Croft Murray 1970, p 154. *See also* I Roscoe 1986.

Andien de Clermont: Decorative Painter to the Leicester House Set, *Apollo* **CXXIII**, February 1986, pp 92–101, which provides a useful account of the painter's career, although the Wilton work is misunderstood in some particulars

62 *Book of Capitols*, Devonshire Collection, Chatsworth. *See also* J Bold 1981. John Webb: Composite Capitals and the Chinese Language, *Oxford Art Journal* **IV**, 1, pp 14–16

63 North's writings were not published until the present century; *see* H M Colvin and J Newman 1981, especially pp 122–41

64 H Wotton 1624. *The Elements of Architecture*, p 57

65 T Fuller 1648. *The Holy State*, 2nd edn, p 156

66 Pratt, like North, remained unpublished until the present century: *see* R T Gunther 1928. *The Architecture of Sir Roger Pratt*, Oxford University Press, p 62

67 WHA, mid eighteenth-century proposal plans

68 WRO, 2057 H5/1

69 E Mercer 1962, p 18

70 A plan in Vertue's collection of antiquarian drawings of *c.* 1725 to *c.* 1735 shows the layout of the sculpture in the west wing, the Hunting Room and the Single and Double Cube Rooms. Bodleian Library, Gough Drawings a1, f14

71 J Harris and A A Tait 1979, no 111

72 Ibid no 65

73 J Kennedy 1786. *A Description of the Antiquities and Curiosities in Wilton House*; W Gilpin 1798. *Observations on the Western Parts of England, Relative Chiefly to Picturesque Beauty*, p 107

74 J Barbet 1633. *Livre d'Architecture, d'Autels, et de Cheminées*

75 WHA, nos 58, 108

76 E Croft Murray 1962, pp 198, 204

77 Sidney, 16th Earl of Pembroke 1968, p 91

78 E Croft Murray 1962, p 198

79 Ibid p 207

80 O Hill and J Cornforth 1966, p 86; M Whinney and O Millar 1957, p 291

81 RIBA Ms CHA 1/13

82 WHA 2057 H1/6

83 J Hanway 1757. *A Journal of Eight Days Journey*, i, 2nd edn, pp 62–4

84 Sidney, 16th Earl of Pembroke 1968 *see also* J Evelyn. *The Diary of John Evelyn*, ed E S de Beer, Oxford University Press, 1959, entry for 20 July 1654

85 WHA, no 56

86 Victoria & Albert Museum, 3436—66, 67; O Hill and J Cornforth 1966, p 86

87 However, the drawings do not appear to fit any of the rooms at Drayton, and it has been suggested that the form of coronet and the devices shown in the drawings indicate a Medici client and therefore could have been drawn for Cosimo III who visited Wilton in 1669. *See* A Laing 1986. In Context, *Country Life* **CLXXIX**, pp 970–1, (reviewing J Harris 1985. *The Design of the English Country House 1620–1920*, Trefoil Books, where the drawings are reproduced on pp 88–9)

88 R Neve 1726. *The City and Country Purchaser and Builder's Dictionary*, p 246 (Facsimile edn, David and Charles, 1969)

89 E Croft Murray, 1970, p 194

90 WHA, no 110. It has not been established whether this is the Thomas Ward who is listed by both M H Grant (*A Dictionary of British Landscape Painters*, F Lewis Publishers 1952), and C Wood. (*The Dictionary of Victorian Painters*, 2nd edn, Antique Collectors' Club, 1978), as being active between 1819 and 1840 as a painter of portraits, genre, still life and landscape

91 E Croft Murray 1970, p 194

92 WHA, 2057 H1/6; mentioned in a letter from Lord Carnarvon to Lord Pembroke

93 *See* J Le Pautre engravings bound in a volume with J Cotelle, *Livre de divers ornemens pour plafonds* . . . Collection of the University of London Library, Senate House, cat 26 d 4

94 Sidney, 16th Earl of Pembroke 1968, p 89

95 WHA, 2057 H3/18

96 E Croft Murray 1962, p 207; 1970, p 194

97 C Fiennes. *The Journeys of Celia Fiennes*, ed C Morris, The Cresset Press, 1947, p 9

98 WHA, 2057 H1/6 and H3/22

99 J Britton 1847, p 88

100 WHA, 2057 H3/21. The inventory is at the WRO, 2057 H5/1

101 WHA. *See also* E Olivier 1944, pp 158–9; C Hussey 1963c, pp 264–7

102 Wilton House, framed survey

103 Sidney, 16th Earl of Pembroke 1968, p 6

104 G Jackson-Stops (ed) 1985. *The Treasure Houses of Britain*, Yale University Press, p 313 (The catalogue of the exhibition at the National Gallery of Art, Washington, where the bust was exhibited)

105 WHA, 2057 H3/22

106 The bathroom had a projecting room attached, probably housing a cistern. When Lord Oxford visited in 1738, he noted that the 9th Earl had made alterations, 'chiefly upon the ground Floor under the Great Apartments wch were Lumber rooms or worse . . . [he has] fitted up the Apartments under the Great Room next to the Gardens extreamly well and by this means he has been able to sort and to Range his Statues . . . etc.' (BL Ms Loan 29/234, fo 64ff)

107 J Hanway 1757. *A Journal of Eight Days Journey*, i, 2nd edn pp 62–4

108 H M Colvin and J Newman 1981, p 128

109 *See also* M W Barley 1967. Rural Housing in England. In *The Agrarian History of England and Wales*, iv, ed J. Thirsk, Cambridge University Press, p 699

110 C Campbell 1717, p 3

111 A Young 1772. *A Six Weeks Tour through the Southern Counties of England and Wales*

112 Bodleian Library, Gough Maps 33, 19r

113 T Martyn 1766. *The English Connoisseur*, ii

114 H M Colvin 1978, p 452

115 Information kindly provided by Mrs S Jeffrey during the course of work on her PhD thesis: *English Baroque*

Architecture – The Work of John James, University of London, 1986

116 E Croft Murray 1970, p 263

117 J Harris 1970, pp 251–2. *See also* J Hanway 1757. *A Journal of Eight Days Journey*, I, 2nd edn, p 64

118 J Harris 1970, pp 251–2

119 WHA, 2057 A5/4

120 W Gilpin 1798. *Observations on the Western Parts of England, Relative Chiefly to Picturesque Beauty*, p 97. Gilpin, the apostle of the picturesque landscape, did not specify his criticisms, but it is apparent from his account that whilst admiring Wilton he felt that 'there are some things . . . yet wanting to give the house an air of magnificence' and its setting also was lacking in picturesque qualities

121 WHA, 2057 H1/6. Wilton was a much visited house. It was the first English house to have a printed guide to its collections; Carlo Gambarini's *Description of the Earl of Pembroke's Pictures*, 1731. This was followed in 1751 by Richard Cowdry's *A Description of the Pictures, Statues, Bustos . . . at Wilton*. The number of houses for which guidebooks were available rose to a peak in the first two decades of the nineteenth century, no doubt as a response to the popularity of travel amongst the gentry and the aristocracy during the picturesque era. John Harris has noted that it was at that time 'an unwritten rule that reasonable access should be permitted', a state of affairs which changed as travel became cheaper in the 1830s and more people could take advantage of the opportunities which it offered. *See* J Harris 1986. The Guide in the Hand, *Country Life* **CLXXIX**, pp 1200–2

122 WHA, 2057 H1/6

123 Quoted by N R Wilkinson 1908. *Wilton House Guide*, p 85

124 WHA, 2057 H3/18

125 J M Robinson 1979. *The Wyatts*, Oxford University Press pp 269, 273

126 WHA, 2057 H1/6

127 *Ibid*

128 WHA, no 108

129 WHA, Letter-book

130 WHA, 2057 H1/6

131 WHA, 2057 H1/13

132 WHA, no 108

133 WRO, 2057 A2/11

134 A Webb chimney-piece, possibly re-sited, survives in this former dining-room

135 Their authorship is unknown: they are certainly not Jamesian in style

136 C Hussey 1963b, pp 314–17

137 The name indicates that it was used originally for the distribution of Abbey alms to the poor

138 Lieutenant Hammond 1635. Description of a Journey, *The Camden Miscellany* **XVI**, 1936, pp 67–8

139 J Britton 1847, p 86

140 WHA, 2057 H3/2

141 The Buckler illustration: WAS, Devizes

142 *The Gentleman's Magazine*, April 1812, p 340

143 WHA, no 108

144 *Survey of the Lands of William, 1st Earl of Pembroke*, (c. 1565) WRO 2057/S3. Privately printed for the Roxburghe Club, 1909, ed C R Straton

145 BL Add 33767B, fo 24. *See also* L Magalotti 1821. *Travels of Cosimo III, Grand Duke of Tuscany, through England, during the reign of Charles the Second*

146 At Wilton House. *See also* Sidney, 16th Earl of Pembroke 1968; J Harris 1979. *The Artist and the Country House*, Sotheby Parke Bernet, p 128

147 C Campbell 1717, pl 67

148 J Harris 1984. An English neo-Palladian episode and its connections with Visentini in Venice, *Architectural History* **27**, pp 231–40

149 WHA, no 109

150 J Britton 1847, p 87

151 C Campbell 1717, pl 66

152 O Hill and J Cornforth 1966, p 183

153 H M Colvin 1954, p 183

154 J Harris and A A Tait 1979, nos 109, 110

155 Ibid nos 112–16

156 Lieutenant Hammond 1635.

Description of a Journey, *The Camden Miscellany* **XVI**, 1936, p 66

157　C Fiennes. *The Journeys of Celia Fiennes*, ed C Morris, The Cresset Press, 1947, pp 9–10

158　D. Defoe 1748. *A Tour thro' the Whole Island of Great Britain*, ɪ, 4th edn, pp 332–6

159　At Wilton House. *See also* Sidney, 16th Earl of Pembroke 1968

160　I de Caus *c.* 1654. *See also* J Harris and A A Tait 1979, nos 113–16

161　C Fiennes. *The Journeys of Celia Fiennes*, ed C Morris, The Cresset Press, 1947, p 9

162　J Britton 1847, p 87

163　Lord Oxford noted that the 9th Earl had 'destroyed the old ridiculous Water Works and whims that were then when made much in vogue. . .' BL Ms Loan 29/234, fo 64ff

164　C Hussey 1963c, p 208

165　C Campbell 1717, pl 65

166　R Strong 1979. *The Renaissance Garden in England*, Thames and Hudson, p 156

167　Bodleian Library, Gough Maps 33, 19r

168　*See* Rocque's plan of the park and garden in 1746, Devizes Museum

169　I de Caus *c.* 1654

170　C Campbell 1717, pl 67

171　Lieutenant Hammond 1635. Description of a Journey, *The Camden Miscellany* **XVI**, 1936, p 67

172　R Strong 1979. *The Renaissance Garden in England*. Thames and Hudson, pp 147–61, 230

173　D Defoe 1748. *A Tour thro' the Whole Island of Great Britain*, ɪ, 4th edn, pp 332–6

174　WHA, no 58

175　Ibid

176　F Haskell and N Penny 1982, p 221

177　WHA, no 108

178　C Hussey 1963c, p 267

179　WHA, 2057 A5/1

180　A Palladio 1570, ɪɪɪ, pp 26–7. *See also* C Hussey, Palladian Bridges in England, *Country Life Annual*, 1962, pp 60–3

181　WHA. *See also* E Olivier 1944, pp 158–9

182　Painting at Wilton House: F Haskell and N Penny 1982, p 254

183　Bodleian Library, Gough Maps 33, 19r and Bodleian Ms Top Gen d 13 fo 10r

184　D Defoe 1748. *A Tour thro' the Whole Island of Great Britain*, ɪ, 4th edn, pp 332–6

185　J Harris 1970, p 252

186　W Gilpin 1798. *Observations on the Western Parts of England, Relative Chiefly to Picturesque Beauty*, p 101

187　WHA, no 108

188　J Harris 1970, p 252

189　C Campbell 1717, pls 61–2

190　P Hetherington 1980. Two Medieval Venetian Well Heads in England, *Arte Veneta* **XXXIV**, pp 9–17

191　J Pope-Hennessy 1964. *Catalogue of Italian Sculpture in the Victoria & Albert Museum*, no 1. I am indebted to Mr Paul Williamson of the Department of Sculpture, Victoria & Albert Museum, for his comments

192　F Ongania 1889. *Raccolta delle vere da pozzo in Venezia*; A Rizzi 1981. *Vere da Pozzo di Venezia*, La Stamperia di Venezia Editrice

193　VCH 1956. *A History of Wiltshire*, ɪɪɪ, Institute of Historical Research, University of London, p 362

194　J Aubrey. *Brief Lives*, ed O Lawson Dick, Penguin Books 1972, p 297

195　WHA, no 35

A Note on the Archives

The Wilton House archives were being recatalogued during the course of research on the house. The new catalogue numbers which apply to the holdings at both Wilton House and the Wiltshire Record Office are prefixed by the number 2057. The complete catalogue of the holdings in both locations can be consulted at the Wiltshire Record Office.

Amesbury Abbey

1　R Colt Hoare 1826. *The Modern History of South Wiltshire* ɪɪ, ɪɪɪ

2　For the early history of the community, see also (*WAM*) **X**, 1867, pp 61–84; *Wiltshire Notes and Queries* **III**, 1901,

p 114 ff; VCH *Wiltshire*, III, 1956,
pp 242–9. For the subsequent history of
the ownership of the house *see* E Kite
1901. In *Wiltshire Notes and Queries*, **III**.
At the time of the surrender of the
Abbey, 4 December 1539, the
community comprised the Abbess, 33
nuns, 4 priests and 33 servants; *see* D
Knowles and R N Hadcock 1971.
Medieval Religious Houses, Longman,
p 105

3   *Wiltshire Notes and Queries* **III**, 1901,
pp 354–5

4   WRO 283/79

5   For this and the subsequent family
history, see *Burke's Peerage and
Baronetage* entry for Somerset. Burke's
Peerage (Genealogical Books), 1980

6   WRO 283/6—1606; lease drawn up
between Hertford and William Allen

7   WAM **V**, 26, p 367

8   WRO 1300/227A and 227B

9   J R Robinson 1895. *Old Q*, cited by Miss
Juliet Allan (*see* note 42)

10   Printed sales particulars: WRO 283/202

11   J Harris, S Orgel and R Strong 1973,
p 207

12   C R Cockerell. *Diary* (RIBA Ms
Collection) edited version published
by J Harris 1971

13   C Campbell 1725; G Vertue, *Notebooks*
II, in *Walpole Society* **XX**, p 32

14   Metropolitan Museum of Art, New
York, no 26.85, fo 167r, 167v,
236r–41r. The staircase balustrade
sketched by Richardson was
published in *The Builder* **II**, 1844, p 563

15   RIBA, W13/16, 2–5

16   RIBA, uncatalogued

17   W Stukeley 1740. *Stonehenge, A Temple
Restor'd to the British Druids*

18   Harrison and Co 1787. *Picturesque Views
of the Principal Seats of the Nobility and
Gentry in England and Wales*

19   R Colt Hoare 1826. *The Modern History
of South Wiltshire*, II, III, The Buckler
drawing is in the Mellon Collection and
there is a photograph of it in the
Wiltshire Archaeological Society
Library, Devizes

20   Devonshire Collection, Chatsworth,
Album 26, no 127

21   The Seymour arms are illustrated and
described in *Wiltshire Notes and Queries*
II, pp 586–7

22   J Summerson 1970, p 146

23   A Palladio 1570, II, p 65

24   Illustrated in W Kent II, 1727

25   J Harris 1972, fig 62

26   C Campbell 1717

27   D Lewis 1981, pp 217–18

28   J Harris 1971

29   J Harris 1970, p 245. *See also* Sir John
Soane's *Lectures on Architecture*, ed A
T Bolton, Soane Museum Publications,
1929

30   J Paine 1767. *Plans, Elevations & Sections
of Noblemen & Gentlemen's House . . .*
pls 33–4 Paine's plans of Amesbury are
mentioned in Sir William Chambers'
correspondence with the Duchess of
Queensberry (Chambers' Letter-
books, BL Add 41134, pp lv–2v, July
1772): 'if a plan of the Duke of
Queensbury's house will be useful to
Sir Wm, Mr Paine can furnish him
with one he having had occasion to
make Plans of the Whole of that
Estate. . . It seems unaccountable to
the Dutchess of Queensbury that Mr
Paine the Duke of Devonshire's Agent
or Survayer the person ordered to
make plans of that whole estate, should
know nothing of five plans framed,
and sent corded up to the Duke of
Devonshire . . . the occasion of the
Dutchesses sending the five plans was
because the Duke of Devonshire
desired leave for his people to view the
house'.
   No such plans are known in the
Devonshire Collection at Chatsworth
today, nor is it known why they were
made, but a possible explanation,
kindly suggested by Dr Peter Leach,
could be that the Queensberrys
intended to raise a mortgage on the
Amesbury estate from the Duke of
Devonshire.

31   J Harris 1971. The main staircase,
'Ascends only to principal 4 bed Ro: &
2 dressg Ro: centre being occupied with
cieling, back stairs then continue to
ascend to lantern & flat at top . . .'

32   S Serlio 1619. *Tutte l'Opere d'Architettura*

et Prospetiva VII, p 149. Reprinted by Gregg International Publishers in 1964

33 *See also* Coke's House, West Burton, Sussex, in *Country Life* **CII**, 1947, pp 926–9

34 J Summerson 1966. The Book of Architecture of John Thorpe, *Walpole Society* **XL**, T45

35 *See* note 31 above. Cockerell noted that the wings of Amesbury were of a later date than the main body of the house but he did not make any comment on the date of the attics

36 R T Gunther 1928. *The Architecture of Sir Roger Pratt*, Oxford University Press p 37

37 H M Colvin and J Newman 1981, pp 62, 129–30

38 J A Gotch 1921. Some Newly Found Drawings and Letters of John Webb, *Journal of the Royal Institute of British Architects* **XXVIII**, 3rd series, p 568

39 Northumberland Ms U III 5, Alnwick

40 Noted at the end of Book VII of Webb's copy of Serlio's *Tutte l'Opere d'Architettura et Prospetiva*, 1619, Collection of the RIBA Library

41 WRO 944/1

42 Drummonds Branch, Royal Bank of Scotland, London; ledgers 1731–61 (This information was provided by Miss Juliet Allan, Principal Inspector, Crown Buildings and Monuments Advisory Group, HBMC. Much of the information which follows, relating to the Flitcroft period, derives from Miss Allan's research and we are grateful to her for making it available to us.)

43 *See also* S Margetson 1985. Sweet Tempered Satirist, *Country Life* **CLXXVIII**, pp 832–3

44 Sir John Clerk's Travel Diary, Clerk of Penicuik Mss, General Register House, Edinburgh; quoted in J Fleming 1962. *Robert Adam and his Circle*, John Murray, p 25

45 J Swift. *Correspondence*, III ed H Williams, Clarendon Press, 1963–5, pp 443–6, 450–2

46 Bodleian Library, MSGD a3* fo 32. *See also* P Willis 1977. *Charles Bridgeman and the English Landscape Garden*, Zwemmer

47 J Swift. *Correspondence*, IV ed H Williams, Clarendon Press, 1963–5, pp 161–3

48 D Defoe 1748. *A Tour thro' the Whole Island of Great Britain,* I, 4th edn, pp 303–4

49 WRO

50 Mrs Elizabeth Montagu 1813. *Correspondence*, III, p 59

51 Wootton also worked for Henry Hoare at Stourhead

52 E Croft Murray 1962, p 266

53 *Wiltshire Notes and Queries* **III**, 1901

54 WRO, Antrobus papers

55 Drummonds Branch, Royal Bank of Scotland, London; ledgers (*see* note 42 above). James Essex made a drawing of the roof structure of the new wing, possibly in 1758, the year in which he was at Salisbury Cathedral making a survey, probably of a roof (BL. Add 6768) *See also* T Cocke 1984. *the Ingenious Mr Essex, Architect,* Fitzwilliam Museum, Cambridge, p 16

56 WRO, 283/204. Cockerell's plan is published in J Harris 1971

57 WRO, 283/129

58 Harrison and Co 1787. *Picturesque Views of the Principal Seats of the Nobility and Gentry in England and Wales*

59 J Britton 1801. *Beauties of Wiltshire* II, pp 148–54

60 *Wiltshire Notes and Queries* **III**, 1901

61 WRO, 283/202

62 *The Builder* **XIV**, 1856, p 481; *Country Life* **XI**, 1902, p 272

63 N Burton 1984. Thomas Hopper and Late Georgian Eclecticism, *Architectural Association Files* **V**, January 1984, p 41

64 Based on examination of the present structure and on the sketch notes made by the architect C Burford in 1979, which survive at Amesbury

65 *See also* R Kerr 1871. *The Gentleman's House*, 3rd edn, p 211: 'The Cook's-Room becomes a necessary adjunct of the Kitchen when a man-cook is kept: it is in fact his official retreat where alone he can reflect upon the mysteries of his art and consult his authorities'.

66 Ibid p 250: 'The ordinary female domestics are usually provided with Bedrooms on the uppermost story, or over the Offices, accessible by the Back-Staircase . . . The ordinary men-servants must have their Sleeping-rooms in a separate quarter . . . When the number of men–servants is sufficiently large, their rooms ought to be approached by a special Staircase, ascending of course from their own side of the Offices'.

67 J Austen, *Northanger Abbey*. Everyman edn, 1906, p 157: 'This passage is at least as extraordinary a road from the breakfast-parlour to your apartment, as that staircase can be from the stables to mine.'

68 The house was not mentioned in the 1851 Census. There is a tradition, the source of which is obscure, that Lady Antrobus and part of the family first slept in the house on the night of 10 October 1859

69 *Wiltshire Notes and Queries* **III**, 1901

70 RIBA, uncatalogued

71 RIBA, uncatalogued. The pencilled measurements on the plan suggest that Cole in 1885 was engaged on work in the long saloon. He is said to have worked also at the house prior to this date: 'the saloon with a large cove was pulled down during alterations under J J Cole, before those of 1853'. (Architectural Publication Society, *The Dictionary of Architecture*, T–Z, 1892, p 25.) This suggests the possibility that Cole was first brought in to continue the programme begun by Hopper, and was then consulted again thirty years later about alterations

72 G Jackson-Stops 1981. Thomas Hopper at Melford and Erddig, *National Trust Studies*

73 At Wilbury there is a half of a four-centred stone doorhead inscribed '–HIS TOWER 1600'. This so closely resembles the doorhead to Diana's House that it suggests that Benson removed it for re-use. It was perhaps originally intended for a doorway into the stair tower

74 *Wiltshire Notes and Queries* **III**, 1901

75 Drummonds Branch, Royal Bank of Scotland, London; ledgers (*see* note 42 above)

76 Bodleian Library, MSGD a3* fo 32

77 WRO, Antrobus Deeds

78 J Allan, unpublished account of Flitcroft's work at Amesbury, kindly made available to RCHME by Miss Allan

79 T Turner. The works of John Smeaton – A Chronological Survey, *Transactions of the Newcomen Society* **50**, 1978–9, p 47

80 R Pococke 1889. *The Travels through England of Dr Richard Pococke*, II, ed J J Cartwright, p 57

81 WRO, 944/1

82 Bodleian Library, MSGD a3* fo 32

83 Andrews' and Dury's map, WRO

84 Published by R Colt Hoare 1826. *The Modern History of South Wiltshire*, II, III; the Buckler drawing is in the Mellon Collection

85 RIBA, W13/16, 5

86 *See also* S Serlio 1619. *Tutte l'Opere d'Architettura e Prospetiva*, VI. Reprinted by Gregg International Publishers, 1964

87 W Kent 1727, pl 60

88 C Campbell 1717, pl 67

89 James Lees-Milne recorded damage by soldiers 'who have destroyed the entrance gates and one of John Webb's gate-piers' on a visit to Amesbury in 1947; J Lees-Milne 1984. *Caves of Ice*, Faber and Faber, p 194

90 But comparable gate-piers, attributed to Inigo Jones, are illustrated in W Kent 1727, I, pl 61

91 J Harris 1970, p 196

92 D Defoe 1748. *A Tour thro' the Whole Island of Great Britain* I, 4th edn, pp 303–4

93 *Wiltshire Notes and Queries* **III**, 1901

94 R Pococke 1889. *The Travels through England of Dr Richard Pococke*, II, ed J J Cartwright, p 57

95 J Hanway 1757. *A Journal of Eight Days Journey*, I, 2nd edn, p 198

96 Chambers' Letter-books, BL Add 41134, pp 13–14

97 *See* note 30

Wilbury House

1 C Hussey 1959, pp 1014–18, 1148–51; C Morris (ed) 1947. *The Journeys of Celia Fiennes*, The Cresset Press, p xv

2 WRO, Antrobus Deeds 283/44; cited by H M Colvin 1978

3 J Summerson 1959, pp 570–87

4 K Woodbridge 1970, p 21

5 WRO

6 WRO, Acc 1408/1

7 WRO, MTD/E/14

8 C Hussey 1959, p 1151

9 C Campbell 1715

10 H E Stutchbury 1967. *The Architecture of Colen Campbell*, Manchester University Press, p 12; H M Colvin 1978

11 H Avray Tipping 1932. Wilbury Park, Wiltshire, *Country Life* **LXXI**, pp 96–102

12 A Palladio 1570, ii, p 58 (The position of the Wilbury staircases is such that they could not have been lit from the cupola)

13 J Harris 1985, *The Design of the English Country House 1620–1920*, Trefoil Books, p 112

14 *Country Life* **LXXI** 1932, p 97; *Country Life* **CXXVI**, 1959, p 1015

15 Engraving by J C Smith, 1813 for J Britton 1814. *The Beauties of England and Wales*

16 VCH 1956. *A History of Wiltshire*, iii, Institute of Historical Research, University of London, p 91

17 *Country Life* **CXXVII**, 1960, p 29

18 J Britton 1825. *Beauties of Wiltshire*, iii, p 340

19 Ibid

20 N Pevsner 1975. *The Buildings of England: Wiltshire*, revised edn by B Cherry, Penguin Books, p 574

21 B Jones 1974. *Follies and Grottoes*, Constable & Co, p 408

22 This is marked on Andrews' and Dury's map of 1773, 2½ miles south–east of Wilbury House

Stourhead

1 For Stourhead, *see* K Woodbridge 1970, pp 17–23; J Harris 1981, p 65. Campbell published his designs for Stourhead in *Vitruvius Britannicus* iii, 1725

2 A Palladio 1570, ii, p 55

3 D Dodd 1979. Rebuilding Stourhead 1902–1906. *National Trust Studies, 1979*, Sotheby Parke Bernet, pp 113–27

4 For the Stourhead landscape, *see* K Woodbridge 1970, pp 24–37; K Woodbridge 1978. *The Stourhead Landscape*, National Trust

5 R Wood 1757. *Ruins of Baalbec*

Tottenham Park

1 J Harris. The Building Works of Lord Viscount Bruce. In *Lord Burlington and his Circle*, papers given at a Georgian Group symposium, 1982, pp 25–51; J Harris 1981, p 71. Three eighteenth-century prospects of Tottenham have been discovered recently; *see* Sotheby's exhibition catalogue, *The Glory of the Garden*, 1987, p 72

2 A Palladio 1570, ii, p 47

3 We might presume that it was Burlington's high regard for Amesbury which lay behind the publication of both its entrance and back fronts in William Kent's *Designs of Inigo Jones*, ii, 1727, after the publication of the entrance front only in Campbell's *Vitruvius Britannicus*, iii, 1725

4 A Palladio 1570, ii, p 68

5 The Earl of Cardigan 1949. *The Wardens of Savernake Forest*, Routledge & Kegan Paul, p 296

6 J Harris. The Building Works of Lord Viscount Bruce. In *Lord Burlington and his Circle*, papers given at a Georgian Group symposium, 1982, p 29

Lydiard Park

1 *Lydiard Park and Church*, guidebook (date unknown), published by Swindon Corporation, based on RCHME investigation (1961) and research for the VCH series. See also *Country Life* **CIII**, 1948, pp 578–81, 626–9

2 H M Colvin 1978, p 562

Glossary

Achievement   An armorial escutcheon

Aedicule   An opening framed by columns or pilasters, and surmounted by a lintel, gable or pediment

Arabesque (*arabesco*)   Flowing, non-figurative linear decoration

Architrave   *see* **Entablature**

Artisan mannerism   A term invented by Sir John Summerson to describe the style of those predominantly brick-built, craftsman-designed houses of the 1630s and onwards, which used classical features in a manner at variance with the precision of the Jonesian court style

Ashlar   Finely cut and finely jointed squared stone, laid in regular, horizontal courses.

Astylar   A façade without columns or pilasters

Baroque   A style which is characterised (in architecture) by the vigorous manipulation of mass, rhythm and space to dramatic and emotive ends. Wren, Hawksmoor, Vanbrugh and Archer were the chief exponents of the English baroque architectural style

Bay   A vertical subdivision of a building, defined by the order, by windows or by vaulting

Belvedere   A turret or lantern on the roof of a house, placed for viewing purposes; it may also be a free-standing structure, in which case the term is interchangeable with **Gazebo**

Bolection moulding   A convex moulding, projecting beyond the surface which it frames

Capital   The head of a column or pilaster, the column comprising, in ascending order: base, shaft and capital

Cartouche   A shaped, ornamental panel, often framed, usually bearing an inscription or heraldic device

Chamfer   The surface formed by the cutting away of the sharp edge of a block of stone, usually at an angle of 45°

Classicism   A revival of the principles of Greek and Roman architecture, often mediated by the influence of the styles of the Italian and French Renaissance

Cornice   *see* **Entablature**

Coving   A large, concave, arched moulding, especially between the ceiling of a room and its cornice; hence 'coved ceiling'

Cupola   A small, domed roof, or a small, domed turret built upon a roof

Double pile   A plan type, increasingly popular throughout the seventeenth century in England; it comprises a rectangular block, two rooms deep, sometimes with a central, lateral corridor

Entablature   In the classical orders, the horizontal members above the capital, comprising, in ascending order, the architrave, frieze and cornice

Gadrooned   Decorated with a series of convex curves

Gazebo   A summerhouse, or turret-like structure on the roof of a house, providing a view in a garden or park. This term is sometimes interchangeable with **Belvedere**

Gothick   A term used to describe the often frivolous eighteenth-century style which attempted to recreate the atmosphere of gothic architecture. Not to be confused with the later, more serious gothic revival

Grotto   An artificial cave, decorated with rock and shell-work, usually incorporating fountains and waterworks

Ha-ha   A ditch or sunk fence which divided the formal garden from the landscaped park in the eighteenth century without interrupting the view

Loggia   A covered gallery, often colonnaded, open to the air on one or more sides

Mullion   A vertical member dividing a window into a number of lights

Neo-Palladianism   *see* p 1

Oeil-de-bœuf   A small, round or oval window

Order   In classical architecture, the column and entablature decorated and proportioned according to one of the accepted modes: Tuscan, Doric, Ionic, Corinthian, Composite

Palladianism   *see* p 1

Parterre   Level area of garden, close to the house, laid out in formal beds

Pediment   A triangular gable above an entablature. It may be straight-sided or curved. It is *broken* when the apex of the triangle is left open and *open* when the base of the triangle is open

Pentice   A roofed, external corridor

Piano nobile   The principal storey of a house, containing the reception rooms, raised above ground level, with a basement or ground floor below

Pilaster   A rectangular column, projecting slightly from the face of the wall; referred to as *reeded* when decorated wih vertical parallel, convex mouldings, and fluted when vertically grooved

Platband   An unmoulded, projecting string course

Porte-cochère   A porch or portico, large enough to admit a carriage

Portico   A roofed colonnade, forming the entrance or centrepiece to a building. If recessed it is *in antis*, with the columns aligned with the façade; if it projects it is *prostyle*

Putto   A chubby, naked boy painted or carved

Quoins   The dressed stones at the external angles of a building

Rococo   A light, fanciful style of interior decoration often asymmetrical and abstract, incorporating shell-like forms, curves and floral motifs. It was popular in England during the middle decades of the eighteenth century

Rustication   Deeply jointed masonry, cut in an emphatic manner to give texture to the wall. It is said to be *frosted* when the surface of the stone is carved to simulate icicles

Scagliola   Cement and colouring matter mixed to imitate marble: in the casing of columns, it is laid on thinly to a plaster coating over a wooden framework

String course   A continuous, horizontal band of brick or stone, set in the surface of an exterior wall

Transom   A horizontal member dividing a window into a number of lights

Wyvern   An heraldic, winged, two-legged dragon with a barbed tail

Select Bibliography

Archer, J 1985. *The Literature of British Domestic Architecture 1715–1842*. Massachusetts Institute of Technology Press

Britton, J (ed) 1847. *The Natural History of Wiltshire*

Burke, J 1976. *English Art 1714–1800*, Clarendon Press

Campbell, C 1715. *Vitruvius Britannicus*, Book I. Reprinted by Benjamin Blom, New York, 1967
1717. *Vitruvius Britannicus*, Book II. Reprinted by Benjamin Blom, New York, 1967
1725. *Vitruvius Britannicus*, Book III. Reprinted by Benjamin Blom, New York, 1967

Caus, I de *c.* 1654. *Wilton Garden*. Reprinted by Garland Publishing, New York and London, 1982

Colvin, H M 1954. The South Front of Wilton House, *Archaeological Journal* **CXI**, pp 181–90
1978. *A Biographical Dictionary of British Architects 1600–1840*, John Murray
1975 (ed). *The History of the King's Works III 1485–1660*, Part I, HMSO
1976 (ed). *The History of the King's Works V 1660–1782*, HMSO
1982 (ed). *The History of the King's Works IV 1485–1660*, Part II, HMSO

Colvin, H M and **Newman, J** (eds) 1981. *Of Building – Roger North's Writings on Architecture*, Oxford University Press

Croft Murray, E 1962. *Decorative Painting in England 1537–1837*, Book I, Country Life Books
1970. *Decorative Painting in England 1537–1837*, Book II, Country Life Books

Cruickshank, D 1985. *A Guide to the Georgian Buildings of Britain & Ireland*, Weidenfeld & Nicolson

Fleming, J, Honour, H and **Pevsner, N** 1980. *Dictionary of Architecture*, Penguin Books

Harris, J 1970. *Sir William Chambers*, Zwemmer
1971. C R Cockerell's 'Ichnographica Domestica', *Architectural History* **14**, pp 5–29
1972. *Catalogue of the Drawings Collection of the RIBA: Inigo Jones and John Webb*, Gregg International
1973. *Catalogue of the Drawings Collection of the RIBA: Colen Campbell*, Gregg International
1981. *The Palladians*, Trefoil Books

Harris, J and **Lever, J** 1966. *Illustrated Glossary of Architecture 850–1830*, Faber & Faber

Harris, J and **Tait, A A** 1979. *Catalogue of the Drawings by Inigo Jones, John Webb and Isaac de Caus at Worcester College, Oxford*, Oxford University Press

Harris, J, Orgel, S and **Strong, R** 1973. *The King's Arcadia: Inigo Jones and the Stuart Court*, Arts Council of Great Britain

Haskell, F and **Penny, N** 1982. *Taste and the Antique*, Yale University Press

Hill, O and **Cornforth, J** 1966. *English Country Houses, Caroline. 1625–1685*, Country Life Books

Hussey, C 1948. The Aesthetic Background to the Art of William Kent. Introduction to M Jourdain, *The Work of William Kent*, Country Life Books, pp 15–24
1955. *English Country Houses, Early Georgian. 1715–1760*, Country Life Books
1959. Wilbury Park, Wiltshire, *Country Life* **CXXVI**, pp 1014–18, 1148–51.
1963a. Wilton House, Wiltshire, *Country Life* **CXXXIII**, pp 1044–8, 1109–13, 1176–80
1963b. James Wyatt and Wilton House, *Country Life* **CXXXIV**, pp 314–17
1963c. Gardens of Wilton House, Wiltshire, *Country Life* **CXXXIV**, pp 206–9, 264–7

Kent, W 1727. *Designs of Inigo Jones*. Reprinted by Gregg International, 1967

Lees-Milne, J 1962. *Earls of Creation*, Hamish Hamilton

Lewis, D 1981. *The Drawings of Andrea Palladio*, International Exhibitions Foundation, Washington DC

Mercer, E 1962. *English Art 1553–1625*, Clarendon Press

Olivier, E 1944. Wilton House 1544–1944 and the Earls of Pembroke, *Country Life* **XCV**, pp 112–15, 156–9

Palladio, A 1570. *I Quattro Libri dell'Architettura*. Reprinted by Ulrico Hoepli Editore, Milan, 1980
1738. *The Four Books of Andrea Palladio's Architecture*. Translated by I Ware. Reprinted by Dover Publications, New York, 1965

Popper, G and **Reeves, J** 1982. The South Front of Wilton House, *Burlington Magazine*, **CXXIV**, June 1982, pp 358–61

Rykwert, J 1980. *The First Moderns: the Architects of the Eighteenth Century*, Massachusetts Institute of Technology Press

Saxl, F and **Wittkower, R** 1948. *British Art and the Mediterranean*. Reprinted by Oxford University Press, 1969

Sidney, 16th Earl of Pembroke 1968. *A Catalogue of the Paintings and Drawings in the Collection at Wilton House*, Phaidon Press

Summerson, J 1959. The Classical Country House in 18th-Century England, *Journal of the Royal Society of Arts*, July 1959, pp 539–87
1966. *Inigo Jones*, Penguin Books
1970. *Architecture in Britain 1530–1830*, Penguin Books

Tait, A A 1964. Isaac de Caus and the South Front of Wilton House, *Burlington Magazine*, **CVI**, February 1964, p 74

Whinney, M and **Millar, O** 1957. *English Art 1625–1714*, Clarendon Press

Willey, B 1934. *The Seventeenth-Century Background*, Chatto & Windus
1940. *The Eighteenth-Century Background*, Chatto & Windus

Wittkower, R 1974. *Palladio and English Palladianism*, Thames and Hudson

Woodbridge, K 1970. *Landscape and Antiquity: Aspects of English Culture at Stourhead 1718–1838*, Clarendon Press

Index